Anonymous

**The history of Ayder Ali Khan, Nabob-Bahader: With historical notes**

New memoirs concerning the East Indies. Vol. 2

Anonymous

**The history of Ayder Ali Khan, Nabob-Bahader: With historical notes**
*New memoirs concerning the East Indies. Vol. 2*

ISBN/EAN: 9783337203924

Printed in Europe, USA, Canada, Australia, Japan

Cover: Foto ©ninafisch / pixelio.de

More available books at **www.hansebooks.com**

# THE HISTORY OF AYDER ALI KHAN,

NABOB-BAHADER:

OR,

New Memoirs concerning the *East Indies.*

WITH HISTORICAL NOTES.

By M. M. D. L. T.

General of Ten thousand Men in the Army of the Mogol Empire, and formerly Commander in Chief of the Artillery of Ayder Ali, and of a Body of European Troops in the Service of that Nabob.

IN TWO VOLUMES.

VOL. II.

LONDON:

PRINTED FOR J. JOHNSON, Nº 72, ST. PAUL'S CHURCH-YARD.

M.DCC.LXXXIV.

# THE HISTORY

OF

# AYDER ALI KHAN:

OR,

# NEW MEMOIRS

CONCERNING

# THE EAST INDIES.

HITHERTO we have given no more than a superficial account of the different wars in which Ayder Ali Khan has been engaged againſt the Marattas, the Engliſh, and other enemies, who envied his ſucceſs, or dreaded his power. The true reaſon why the former actions of this ce-lebrated

lebrated conqueror have not been given in a more ample manner in the prefent work, is, that the Author, not having joined the army of the Nabob before the time of the war on the coaft of Malabar, did not think it necef- fary to fpeak largely concerning military ope- rations he could only know from the commu- nications of others. Every perfon acquainted with fubjects of this nature, muft be fenfible how very imperfect an idea of the particulars of any war can be gathered from the accounts of officers, who, engaged in their own duty, cannot have much opportunity to contemplate the general fcene of action.

To difplay the character, the genius, and the talents of Ayder, with regard to the art of war, it would doubtlefs have been highly in- terefting to have defcribed all the marches, fieges, and battles, in which he has exerted himfelf. But the curiofity of the reader will be amply fatisfied in the following volume, by the details given of facts that happened during the war between Ayder and the Englifh. The Author will at leaft relate what he has feen, and clearly come to the knowledge of; with
the

the assurance that this, of all the wars in which Ayder has been engaged, is the best adapted to make known the great abilities of that Nabob; because in this he had to contend with enemies who possessed the superior advantage of the military science and discipline. It will be easy to judge, from the war between the years 1767 and 1769, of the probable event of the present war, which commenced in 1779.

The war we are about to relate is so much the more interesting, as it forms an epoch in the history of the Europeans in India; since it is the first war the Europeans have finished by asking peace of the Indians.

Before we begin our account of the operations of this famous war, it will be proper to give a display of the forces of the respective combatants.

The possessions of Ayder in the year 1767, when he began the war against the English, consisted of the kingdom of Mayssour; the country of Benguelour, that formerly composed part of Mayssour; all the country called Malleam, or the Carnatic, in the charts, which words signify, in two different languages, the Country of Mountains, and which comprehends all the vallies and mountains from Ambour to Madura, Travancor, and the coast of Malabar; the town of Scirra; the country of Ballapour; the little kingdom of Bisnagar; the kingdom of Canara, which extends from Cape Rama northwards along the frontier of Visapour; and lastly, the sovereignty of the coast of Malabar and the Maldive Islands, these countries being only tributaries. It may be seen, by the chart annexed to this work, that the dominions of Ayder have the advantage of being connected together, and of being defended, on the part of the English, by mountains and narrow entrances. These countries contain, if popular report may be credited, above a thousand fortresses, of different magnitudes; a number, perhaps, beyond the truth: however, as an eye-witness, I can affirm them to be very many. All the large fortresses or garrisons are guarded by the troops of the army, which are changed from time to time; and by garrison soldiers, who are a kind of militia, and serve for less pay than the regular

gular troops. The smaller fortresses are maintained only by this latter order of military; and, in case of any alarm, the inhabitants of the mountains take arms, throw themselves into the forts, and defend them with obstinacy sufficient to require a siege. These fortresses, which seem to have been constructed to defend the country against the incursions of the Marattas, have trenches, and bastions or towers: many of them have their revetement of stone or brick; but the greater part, especially in the flat country, have their embankments of red earth, which possesses the property of acquiring, in a short time, the hardness of bricks baked in the sun. They are all kept in the best repair, or at least have been, ever since they became the property of Ayder.

The dominions of this prince abound in rice, and every other necessary of life, as well as in cattle of every kind; that is to say, oxen, sheep, goats, and elephants. As to the horses and camels, they are for the most part brought out of other countries; and Ayder, by making a proper use of his money, is always provided with a great number of horses and elephants, the moſt uſeful animals in war. He has always a reſerve of theſe in the villages, to the number of three hundred elephants, and from fifteen to twenty thouſand horſe. To be always provided with a ſupply of theſe very neceſſary animals, he never fails to purchaſe all that are offered to him, provided they be robuſt and ſtrong, and the owners will part with them for the price he ſets upon them, after a ſtrict examination; and, as his offers are very equitable, dealers come to him from all parts, to preſent the fineſt of theſe animals for his inſpection.

To all theſe means and inducements that might lead the Nabob to enter into a war with the Engliſh, we may add the aſſurance he had that the Engliſh, being almoſt without cavalry, could not prevent his army from being ſupplied with proviſions from all parts of his dominions: and above all the immenſe treaſures he poſſeſſed, which, joined to the conſiderable revenues of his kingdoms and ſtates, put him in a ſituation to ſupport with eaſe the moſt long and expenſive war. In the year we ſpeak of (1767) all the forces of Ayder Ali Khan

Khan were estimated at about one hundred and eighty or two hundred thousand men, of which twenty-five thousand were cavalry: but, as it was necessary to garrison all the fortresses, and leave some troops on the frontiers, the army he led against the English might be from fifty to fifty-five thousand men; of which eighteen thousand were cavalry, namely, ten thousand of excellent cavalry, and about eight thousand Marattas, Pandaris, and others, that cannot be better compared than to the Cossacks who follow the Russian army, being fit for no service but to ravage the country, or rob the baggage of an army. The infantry consisted of twenty thousand Topasses, or Seapoys, armed with sixteen thousand good firelocks, because all the officers, down to the corporals, have no musquets; besides, this being the custom in the Indian armies, Ayder was not in possession of a sufficient number of good musquets to arm his troops better: they who were left in garrison, were armed with an inferior kind, with wooden ram-rods. The rest of the infantry were Peadars, Carnates, or Caleros, armed with matchlocks and lances.

The number of Europeans was about seven hundred and fifty. They were divided into two companies of dragoons or hussars, two hundred and fifty cannoniers, and the officers and serjeants dispersed among the regiments of grenadiers and Topasses.

There were likewise some troops, armed with arms either unknown or out of use at present in Europe, to the number of about one thousand men, mounted two and two on running camels, having each a firelock of a great length, that threw a ball of about three ounces to a prodigious distance. These arms have an iron rest fixed to the barrel; and the soldiers, who are excellent marksmen, follow the cavalry, and plant themselves in covered places to flank the enemy, among whose cavalry they keep up a very destructive fire. This body of troops have the singular privilege of an ensign for every ten men; whether it be an honour, or a piece of policy to deceive the enemy into an opinion, from the number of standards, that they are opposed by a numerous corps of infantry. The troop is very ancient, being, according to all appearance,

ance, the first among the Indians that bore fire-arms. The same number, of about one thousand or twelve hundred men, carried rockets or fusees of iron, which are boxes of plate iron, made in the form of fusees, and attached to direction rods: they are of various sizes, some containing more than one pound of powder or composition, and fly to the distance of a thousand yards. Many of these rockets are charged to burst; others are sharpened at the end; and others are pierced at the foremost end, being charged so that the wind acts strongly on the flame, and sets fire to the matters it may strike in its course. This implement is, on the whole, far more expensive than useful; which, I suppose, chiefly arises from the want of care and attention in making them up: however they have been sometimes productive of dreadful effects, by setting fire to \* ammunition waggons. These rockets

---

\* According to the relation given by the English of the battle gained by Ayder against the colonels Baylie and Fletcher, a rocket having set fire to an ammunition

rockets are very well adapted for setting fire to towns and villages in which the enemy have magazines. A body of cavalry, not used to this kind of instrument, would be quickly thrown into disorder by it; for the rockets falling at the feet of the horses, emit a flame resembling that of a forge furnace, which frightens them; and when they burst, they do considerable mischief. It is no small advantage, that they describe a curve line, and may therefore be thrown by people that are covered by a line of infantry. The English made use of them against the cavalry of Ayder; but, as it was habituated to the fire by various exercises performed with paper rockets, the horses, instead of being frighted, marched fiercely over them.

A troop of Arabs, armed with bows and arrows, arrived at Syringpatnam a short time

ammunition waggon, which in blowing up set fire to two others, the battle was lost; because Tipou Saeb, son of Ayder, with his cavalry, fell upon the English infantry, which the explosion had thrown into disorder.

before

before the departure of the army. The men were well-made, strong, and active; but, as Ayder did not suppose the arms they bore would have much effect on the enemy, he formed them into two companies; one clothed in red, which he joined to his Savari; and the other, in blue, he gave to the commandant of Europeans, to apply to any service he might think proper. They were very adroit in killing birds and game with their bows and arrows, which were large, and very much ornamented.

The army of Nizam Daulla, Suba of Decan, King of Golconda, &c. was reckoned one hundred thousand strong; but he had not more than forty thousand fighting men, of which thirty thousand were cavalry, and ten thousand infantry. Scarcely two thousand of the infantry were armed with firelocks; the rest had only that kind of musket that is called Cailletaux in India. The infantry was, however, commanded by a brave man, named Abderaman Khan, who had served under Messrs. Bourdonnaye and Bussi. This last caused him to be promoted to the command

he

he possessed. He was very sensible of the bad state of his troop, which was besides very ill paid.

The cavalry was good, but much better for shew than service; every chief being proprietor and absolute master of his own troop. Following the army, for the most part, only as vassals of the empire, they were very little disposed to risque their life and their cattle in any war, except when animated by the desire of revenge, the hope of plunder, or some other passion.

These chiefs were the most powerful lords of Decan; such as Ram Schander, a Maratta prince, who bears the name of Alexander, his supposed or pretended ancestor; the three Nabobs or Patane princes of Sanour, Carpet, and Canour, &c.

The army was followed by a multitude of merchants, working tradesmen, women, and servants, which occasioned the camp to be vastly extended; and would have rendered it an easy matter for the English to surprise it, if Ayder had been possessed of less experience and vigilance. The army of the Suba, though capable of doing very little service in actual war, added vastly to the reputation of Ayder, and might have procured him many allies; but the well-founded suspicions he entertained against Rocum Daulla, and even against Nizam, obliged him to be on his guard against a stroke of perfidy, that would have been of more consequence to him than the loss of a battle. Besides, an indifference and coolness very soon arose between the two Subas, by reason of the continual wants of Nizam and all his chiefs; and Ayder was not disposed to comply with their repeated requests for money, left he should by that means lose both his money and his allies. He moreover repented that he had not previously agreed that Nizam, after having given the investiture of the Nabobship of Arcot to his son, should return to his states. It will be seen, in future, that these allies very soon separated from each other.

The united army possessed a very considerable train of artillery, consisting of at least one hundred and ten pieces of large cannon. That of Ayder was more numerous, better provided

vided with ammunition, better mounted, and served by good European cannoniers; but, out of sixty pieces of cannon, he had thirty of iron. The artillery of Nizam, on the contrary, was all fine European brass cannon; and thirty, at least, were French pieces, cast in the reign of Louis XIV.; being the remaining artillery of the squadron of M. de la Haye, which was lost in a hurricane in the road of Masulipatam: this port then belonged to the Kings of Golconda, Subas of Decan, who recovered the cannon of the sunken vessels, which has by succession come into the hands of Nizam Daulla. This beautiful artillery was ill provided with ammunition, badly mounted, and served by Lascars, or Indian gunners, who are usually cowardly and unskilful.

Ayder likewise employed in this war a small army of about six thousand men, returned from the coast of Malabar. He entrusted the command of this detachment to Maffous Khan, a man who he knew had no pretensions to military skill; but, in his opinion, able to cause the people of Madura, whose sovereign he was, to revolt. This able negociator and keen politician was, however, unfortunate in the attempt to become a warrior; for Colonel Beck, a German in the service of the English, pretending to fly before him, enticed him into the center of Madura, and succeeded in taking him prisoner.

We do not reckon the fleet of Ayder among his forces: it was then composed of an old ship purchased of the Danes, pierced for sixty guns, but furnished with no more than fifty; three others of twenty-four, or thirty-two guns; seven or eight *palms*, vessels both for rowing and sailing, and carrying twelve or fourteen guns; and about twenty *galivats*, or large galliots, carrying eighty men, and two cannons. Three or four of the English company's frigates, that are always ready armed in the Indian sea, would have been sufficient to have dispersed this little fleet. An Englishman, whom Ayder had appointed his admiral, having carried the large vessel to Bombay to refit, it was seized, and declared good prize, as soon as the commencement of hostilities

was

was known: an action that Ayder has always regarded as perfidious on the part of the English.

The power of the English in India was in its meridian in the year 1767. That nation possessed the whole of Bengal, the richest, the most fertile, and the most populous of all the provinces in the empire; the number of its inhabitants being estimated at nine millions when it fell into the hands of the English; but since reduced to six millions, at most, by their vexatious and barbarous government. Besides this province, they possessed all the coasts of Orixa and Coromandel, having no other limits inland than the gates, or mountains; the large towns of Surat and Cambaya, the former of which is the most trading port of all India; the island of Bombay, and the country of Salsete, on the Maratta frontier; the forts of Tillicherry, Mondeli, and Anzingue, on the coast of Malabar; besides a number of factories and different establishments, such as are on the island of Sumatra, too remote to be of any advantage in the present war. The territorial

torial revenues of all these possessions exceeded two hundred millions of French money *, as the Author of these Memoirs is well assured; having had in his hands the state of the English Company's affairs, which was given to the king of England and his Privy Council.

The forces of the English in India were more than ninety thousand men: namely, eight regiments of English infantry, of one thousand men each; three on the establishment of Madras, three on that of Bengal, and two on that of Bombay; besides twelve hundred men forming the artillery companies on the several establishments; and one thousand or twelve hundred invalids in garrison at various places. The Indian troops consisted of sixty-four regiments of one thousand Seapoys each; of which thirty were on the establishment of Madras. Their cavalry might be estimated at about four thousand horse, twelve hundred only being on the Madras establishment. All this cavalry was Indian, except about four

---

* In round numbers, about 8,700,000 *l.* sterling.

hundred Europeans. General Smith, after leaving the neceſſary garriſons, had at his diſpoſal five thouſand Europeans, two thouſand five hundred Seapoys, two thouſand five hundred horſe, including two hundred Europeans; twelve hundred Indians, taught the Engliſh exerciſe, and commanded by European officers. The remainder of his army contained the cavalry of Mehemet Ali Khan; a troop not only much inferior in number to that of Ayder, but even unfit to face the cavalry of that ſovereign, by reaſon of their want of diſcipline, and the bad ſtate of the horſe.

The Engliſh have never yet ſucceeded in the attempt to form a good troop of European horſe in India. As they have ſent a regiment of dragoons from England, it is probable that their arrival may place the affair on another footing. Though it may not immediately be conceived, the reaſon of the want of ſucceſs in forming their intended troop of horſe, conſiſted in the good diſcipline to which they were deſirous of ſubjecting them.

The excellence of the Engliſh cavalry is ſufficiently acknowledged in Europe; and its advantages

vantages confist less in the goodness of the horse, than in the choice of the horsemen. The pay of a horseman in England is such as renders his situation very eligible; so that the sons of rich farmers and tradesmen are very desirous of entering into the service. This being the case, it is in the power of the officers to select handsome, well-formed men, of good character, and to keep them in good discipline merely by the fear of being dismissed. The officers who were first entrusted with the formation of a body of cavalry in India, thought to establish and preserve the same discipline among them, without attending to the great difference of time, place, and persons. The recruits sent from England to India are in general libertines, and people of bad character: and, as the Company will not dismiss a soldier, all the punishment inflicted on a horseman is, to reduce him to serve in the infantry; so that a man is no sooner put among the cavalry, than he is sent back again to his former station. The French have succeeded in forming very good cavalry in India, by attending more to their horsemanship, and less to their discipline and manners.

The English at Madras, in addition to all these troops, in number above thirty thousand [*], had the disposition of the troops of Mehemet Ali Khan; with those of some Palleagars, and of Morao, a Maratta chief; which all together might be about twenty thousand men. The whole army to be employed in the defence of Arcot was consequently at least fifty thousand men; and Ayder was likewise under the necessity of marching in person against eight thousand troops on the Bombay establishment, who attacked him at Mangalor, the centre of his kingdom of Canara.

General Smith had the advantage of possessing an army for the most part better disciplined, and more practised in their evolutions, than that of Ayder; with a numerous corps of Europeans, capable alone, as was generally

[*] There is some error either in this number, or in the enumeration page 18, as they do not agree together. T.

believed

believed before this war, of beating the twelve hundred thousand men which Mehemet Sha, emperor of the Mogols, opposed against Nadir Sha, king of Persia *. His artillery was served by a sufficient number of officers and men, bred up in the service: in short, he had officers and engineers of every kind to second him; and was himself certainly much superior to Ayder in military knowledge. With all these advantages, and a superiority of double the number of firelocks, he was certain of

---

* This way of thinking among the Europeans was partly occasioned by the attack of the army of Nazerzing, above three hundred thousand strong, by eight hundred French, commanded by M. de la Touche. The courage of this small French army, and still more of their general, is not perhaps to be parallelled in any history either ancient or modern. But the success that attended their attempt, on that glorious day which decided the fate of an empire, is due to the policy of M. Dupleix, and the treachery of the chiefs and ministers of Nazerzing; in the same manner as the success of Nadir Sha originated in the intelligence he held with Nizam El Moulouc, the Grand Viûr, and other chiefs of the Mogol army.

gaining every battle, in which the nature of the place, or the post he might take, was such as to prevent the cavalry of Ayder from acting to advantage.

The advantages of General Smith over Ayder were balanced by very great disadvantages: namely, first, the inferiority of his cavalry, which obliged him to reduce the theatre of war as much as possible to the mountainous country: secondly, the impossibility of his preventing the cavalry from ravaging the country, and cutting off his convoys: thirdly, the very great difficulty of procuring a sufficient number of oxen for the conveyance of his artillery, ammunition, and baggage; a difficulty of such importance, that it reduced him to the necessity of having an inferior train of artillery, and to spare his provisions and stores beyond what would otherwise have been necessary. But the greatest embarrassment he suffered consisted in his dependance on the Governor and Council of Madras; who, without having any well-founded knowledge of the forces of Ayder, either with respect to number or discipline—and who, at the same time

time ignorant of the nature of the country, were inceffantly giving orders contrary to his views, and every rational principle of war; and even went fo far as to reproach him for the ravages made by Ayder's cavalry, though, in his advice to them previous to the commencement of the war, he had predicted this confequence to them. And as thofe gentlemen never loft fight of the occafions for enriching themfelves, they fupplied the army by means of contractors, with whom they were in league; treating the inhabitants of Madras in the moft vexatious and odious manner, under pretence of furnifhing the army with neceffaries *.

Though

* Two fingular methods of plundering were invented upon this occafion. The firft was, that inftead of fupplying the troops with arrack, an article eafily procured over all the country, it was thought proper to give them rum; becaufe it could be had only from Batavia, and confequently afforded means of enriching thofe who were concerned in procuring it. The fecond related to the fupplying the army with beafts of carriage. As no one could be found who would

Though we have spoken of the departure of General Smith to take possession of several places in the dominions of Ayder, we have not hitherto spoken of his operations; our intention being to unite all the military opera-

would engage to furnish the army with oxen for the artillery, baggage, &c. they took them by force from the inhabitants; but, instead of paying for them at the rate of six or eight pagodas, their real value, they took them on hire, at a pagoda per month. At the end of the first month, they paid the owner a pagoda; but on the expiration of the second, they informed him that his beast was dead. The ox thus obtained out of the hands of its proprietor, was passed to the account of the Company, as purchased at its full value; though, by this infamous manœuvre, it cost no more than a pagoda. If the proprietor had chosen to have sent a servant with his ox, he must have paid him five rupees per month, instead of three and a half, which is the value of the pagoda of Madras. By the operation of this happy project, the country was soon stripped of all its cattle; no one chusing to purchase any, for the purpose of seeing themselves robbed with impunity. In consequence of this, the greater part of the army necessaries were obliged to be carried by men.

tions of this interesting war in one continued narration. The English General made several sieges during the time of the preparations and negociations of Ayder. He took Tripetour, Vaniambari, and Singueman, without much difficulty; that is to say, each of these ill-fortified places held out some days. He likewise took Caveripatnam, whose fortress did not yield till seventeen days after the trenches were opened; and he besieged Kisnagari, a fortress on a steep mountain, where he was obliged to raise the siege, after having made two assaults; in the last of which he lost twenty-four grenadiers, besides soldiers. This was the only place defended by an European officer *.

It

* The name of this officer was Constantin, a native of Andernac on the Rhine, in the electorate of Cologn. He came to India with Ficher's troop, in 1754; and married a Portuguese, by whom he had a very beautiful daughter: he was serjeant when M. Hughel commanded the Europeans in Ayder's army. The officers discovered that, together with his wife, he was in treaty with the Nabob about selling his daughter; they regarded this transaction as an infamous

It was during the siege of this place that the armies of Ayder and Nizam began to move towards the enemy. Kisnagari is twenty-two leagues from Benguelour, by the road

famous piece of busines, that would disgrace all the Europeans in the army. M. Hughel sent for him, to enquire concerning the design laid to his charge, which he denied. A young officer in the army offered to espouse the girl; and the father received the proposal with gratitude. M. Hughel, in favour of the marriage, at the same time promoted the father: but that very night the parents sold their daughter to Ayder, for fifty thousand rupees; and Ayder sent them into the country of Benguelour. Constantin has ever since that time lived at a distance from the army. After the brave defence of the fortress of Kisnagari, the inhabitants of the flat country brought their most valuable effects, and deposited them in the place for security: he opened the boxes and cabinets, taking out the richest property, to a vast amount, and escaped to Goa; from whence he went to Bombay, and afterwards to Europe. Ayder's French surgeon affirms, that the girl has since told him that she esteemed herself fortunate in being sold to the Nabob; as her father and mother might have made a more shameful traffic with her, if she had staid with them.

*that*

that can be taken by an army; and, in order to arrive at this latter place, it is neceſſary to go through narrow paſſes, which are very eaſily defended.

Ayder directed his march ſo that, at the end of the ſecond day, he found himſelf four leagues from the foot of the mountains; being oppoſite the paſs of Vailour, which opens about four leagues from Caveripatnam, a town and fortreſs on the Paler, ſeven leagues from the paſs of Kiſnagari, which was on the right, and about ſix leagues from the paſs of Ventigheri, which is about two leagues and a half from Vaniambari. No precaution was taken to prevent the Engliſh general from being adviſed of the departure of the army from Benguelour; and conſequently he was ſoon adviſed of that event, as well by his ſpies as by ſecret informers he paid in the army of Nizam.

General Smith, on receipt of this advice, raiſed the ſiege of Kiſnagari, and poſted himſelf to defend the paſs of Vailour; and that with ſo much the more reaſon, as it was the only paſſage through which artillery could be conveyed;

conveyed; and being in the centre, with Caveripatnam in his rear, he was better situated to repair to the defence of the pass Ayder might attempt; or to retire in safety, if necessary.

Ayder convened a council of war, at which Rocum Daulla assisted. Its object was, to decide which of the three passes they should attempt to force; and in order that every one might form an opinion with sufficient knowledge of the business, he produced charts of the different passages, in which every particular was exactly delineated. The council decided, that as the English were posted with all their forces to guard the pass of Vailour, it was proper to issue forth by that of Ventigheri; the pass of Kisnagari being absolutely impracticable for artillery: and though the army of Nizam, by reason of its being encamped to the left of Ayder's forces, was nearer this pass, yet Ayder, according to the agreement, undertook to form the advanced guard with his army. In consequence, orders were given to march at two in the morning, in a single column, leaving all the baggage in the camp.

The

The Carnates, and other irregular troops, formed the head of the column; who were followed by all the Seapoys, each preceded by the grenadiers, and followed by the horse. The artillery came next, led by two thousand Topasses, their grenadiers, and the European cannoniers. And lastly, two companies of European cavalry closed the march, and completed the column. Ayder, at the head of two thousand horse, marched on the right flank of the column.

The English being informed of the order and direction of this march, moved to oppose Ayder, and to gain the pass of Ventigheri before him: a thing easily done, as they had but three leagues to pass over. But it was an unexpected manœuvre to them, when, after an hour's march, the Europeans, the grenadier Topasses, and successively the artillery and all the other Topasses, made a turn to the right, and marched for the pass of Vailour with the utmost celerity.

As this troop was supposed to have no other destination than to escort the artillery, it was contrived, in the course of the march, that there

there should be a considerable interval between them and the cavalry that preceded the Topasses, in order that this counter-march might be less perceived; the chief of the Europeans, who had the command of this part of the army, being alone entrusted with the secret *. The stratagem succeeded perfectly well. The hussars and dragoons passed full speed through the pass, which is long, narrow, and winding, but very even ground. They were followed by the European cannoniers, and the grenadier Topasses, who ran with great expedition,

* When the army was commanded to hasten its march, on the news that the Europeans had taken possession of the pass of Vailour, a surgeon of the army, thinking to do wonders, took the opportunity of a Patmar going from Mahé to Pondicherry, to write to the governor of that place: " We are in full " march to descend to the coast. Our commandant, " who serves as a guide to the armies, has forced a " passage by the strait of Vailour." The Patmar having no reason to avoid the English army, General Smith took this paper from him, and sent it to the governor of Madras. It has since been used as an authentic piece to shew the connection between the French governor and Ayder Ali Khan.

though

though they had already marched quickly over an interval of four leagues. General Smith had been careful to leave some of the infantry of Mehemet Ali, and a party of Indian horse, at the entrance of this pass; but a body of Ayder's cavalry, that had passed the strait of Kisnagari, having appeared in the plain, followed by the garrison of that fortress, the troops left by the English abandoned the pass, and retired with great haste to Caveripatnam. At the instant the European commandant cleared the pass, he met Bahoud Khan *, commander

---

* Bahoud Khan was a Patane chief, that escaped the massacre, caused by Anaverdi Khan, of the Patanes in the service of the Nabob of Arcot. All his family perished; and himself and his brother escaped only on account of their youth. Their mother having retired with them to Pondicherry, M. Dupleix afterwards gave him a commission to raise a body of cavalry in the service of France; and he became commandant of the Indian cavalry. M. Dupleix employed and encouraged this Patane, who has exerted himself on all occasions to shew his attachement to the French. He quitted the service of Nizam Ali Khan to pass into that of Ayder. This Nabob one day

commander of cavalry, who came himself to acquaint him that he found no opposition. On this news he gave orders to fire nine cannon, three and three; the signal agreed

day said to him, " I wonder, Bahoud Khan, that
" you, who had above fifteen hundred horse when in
" the French service, have no more than three hun-
" dred at present." " My Lord," replied the other,
" whenever M. Dupleix said to me, Bahoud Khan,
" you must augment your cavalry, he always added,
" Go to my treasurer, and he will advance the money
" you want." These words were directed at Ayder, who never pays any thing to his cavalry till they have passed in review before him; however, he took no notice; but replied, " You are always so highly at-
" tached to the French, who yet are much in your
" debt, and do not seem to think of paying you,
" though Pondicherry is re-established." " If it had
" not been for the friendship and confidence of the
" French," answered the chief, " I should have had
" nothing, after being robbed of every thing by
" Anaverdi Khan; and if the French have occasion
" for my service, I shall be ready to sacrifice what I
" have left, and my life too." This attachment of him, and many other Indians, has been produced by the great talents M. Dupleix possesses for government.

between

between him and Ayder that the pafs was free. On this fignal, the Nabob caufed his whole army to march to the pafs of Vailour, where he arrived himfelf, at the head of his cavalry, and faw the artillery advance, under the conduct of the Topaffes.

General Smith was foon informed that Ayder's army was advancing through the pafs of Vailour, and retired as quickly as poffible to Caveripatnam; where he did not think it expedient to ftay, but, leaving twelve hundred of his beft Seapoys, fome Topaffes belonging to the artillery, and thirty European cannoniers, he retired to Tripetour, to be nearer affiftance, and at hand to receive the convoys he expected from Madras, as well as to join a body of feven or eight thoufand men, commanded by Colonel Wood, who was then employed in befieging the fortrefs of Ahtour, a very ill-fortified place, defended by Carnates; againft which, however, he employed fifteen days, from the opening his trenches to the time of its furrender. General Smith, when he retired, left one hundred Indian horfemen, to bring him intelligence of the events that might happen in his abſence.

The whole army and artillery of Ayder cleared through the paſs in the courſe of the day, but the baggage and proviſions came through in the night; ſo that the Europeans in the army, who had marched from day-break till night, and were fatigued, as well by that as by hunting (the country abounding with game) were not very well ſatisfied, at night, to be obliged to eat their game, roaſted as well as they could, without bread or rice, to the great diverſion of Ayder, who in vain adviſed them to wait for the cooks.

Ayder had no ſooner paſſed the mountains with his cavalry, than he diſpatched his brother-in-law, Moctum, with four thouſand horſe, to purſue the Engliſh army, and inveſt Caveripatnam.

This order was executed with ſo much diligence and addreſs, that Caveripatnam was inveſted, as well as all the avenues leading to the Engliſh camp at Tripetour, without it being poſſible for General Smith to receive

ceive any advice by the hundred horsemen left in the neighbourhood of Caveripatnam, who were driven into the town. All the Algaras * were interrupted, and the letters being carried to Ayder, convinced him that his suspicions of the correspondence between General Smith and many of the chiefs of Nizam's army, were but too well founded.

Moctum, after leaving the care of the investment of Caveripatnam to another commander, hastened to the environs of Tripetour, and arrived during the night behind the small mountains or rocks that lie about a league from that place. General Smith, who arrived at his camp the second evening of his march, supposed the inactivity of Ayder to be the cause that he had received no news, either from the commander at Caveripatnam, or his friends in Nizam's army. In this persuasion he permitted the servants, with the greatest part of the oxen belonging to the army, to go in search of forage the next

---

* Algaras are couriers on foot or on dromedaries. Those on foot are usually Bramins.

morning.

morning. As soon as Moctum saw them dispersed in the plain, he detached some Pandaris, or irregular cavalry, who quickly threw them into terror and disorder. This was of course observed from the camp and fortress, and the piquets of cavalry, consisting of about one thousand horse, were dispatched to chase the pillagers; who, according to their orders, and usual custom, fled, on perceiving the enemy, and saved themselves by taking the road near which the ambuscade was. The English cavalry were no sooner within reach than Moctum fell upon them, and, having put them to flight, pursued them with so much spirit, that a party being prevented from reaching the camp, and endeavouring to take refuge in the town, the cavalry of Moctum entered with them, and took the place, in spite of the fire from the fort. General Smith, who, on sight of the enemy's cavalry, had hastened to draw up his forces in order of battle, was apprehensive of being surrounded by the cavalry of both armies, and consequently of being obliged to cut his way through, in order to procure provisions and reinforcements;

reinforcements; he therefore collected as many oxen, and as much baggage, as the circumstances would permit, and marched in three columns, his artillery and baggage forming the middle column; and, leaving the fortress of Tripetour, hastened to Singueman, situated at the beginning of a chain of small mountains, transversal to the great mountains passing by Tirnmale and abutting at Gingi. He arrived in safety, though much harrassed by Moctum, who took many oxen loaded with baggage, and about two hundred horsemen, with their horses, of which six only were Europeans.

This irruption of Moctum, and the total want of every kind of advice respecting the operations of Ayder, ought to have given General Smith a very different opinion concerning the military skill and judgment of this Indian warrior, in comparison to those with whom he had hitherto fought: but, considering that Ayder could not come to him without besieging Caveripatnam or Vaniambari, places whose garrisons might have interrupted his convoys, and being at Singueman,

man, distant from Tirnmaly only five leagues, by a road advantageous for infantry, (besides possessing the advantage of his camp being defended by the fortress, a large tank or pond, and the river) he determined to wait the arrival of Colonel Wood; for which purpose he wrote to the council at Madras, to order the junction of the two armies.

Ayder, the evening after he had passed the strait of Vailour, encamped about a league and a half from Caveripatnam, which was invested by his cavalry. He immediately repaired to a mountain at a small distance, from whence he could observe every thing that passed in the town. It was easy to perceive, from the burning of the houses that would have favoured their approach to the fortress, that they intended to abandon the town, and retire into this last place. Ayder, in consequence, gave orders to the commandant of his artillery, to get every thing in readiness for scaling the walls by the Caleros, the Carnates, and other irregular troops, to prevent the English from carrying their effects from the town to the fortress. This officer, who had brought

thirty

thirty pieces of cannon behind the mountain, caused eight to be drawn across the plain, to the very edge of the ditch, in spite of the fire of three pieces of cannon the English had left on the ramparts of the town, after carrying the other pieces into the fortress, whose fire could not incommode them, because masked by the walls of the town. The English commandant was so far from expecting this attack, that, in order to see Ayder's horse more at his ease, he had seated himself with his officers in a tent on the ramparts, at a table covered with bottles. To engage his attention, the eight pieces of cannon, escorted by three battalions of grenadiers and some gunners, marched directly to the gate on the side remotest from the fortress; and, having placed them opposite the gate, they made their first discharge at the tent of the commandant, and immediately overthrew it: after which they directed them against the gate, and the towers that defended it. The troops that had escorted the artillery laid themselves flat on the earth behind the hedges and walls, and in the trenches of the gardens.

It was about two in the afternoon that this cannonade began. During this time, about ten thousand, and as many volunteers *, out of all the troops of the two armies, appeared scattered in the plain, and hiding themselves among the gardens and houses that had been abandoned. The English officers, who had never beheld a scene of this sort before, supposed that this multitude, arriving without musquets, had no other intention than to rob, or to seek for garden-stuff round the town. They imagined that the attack would be made at the breach, and that there would be sufficient time to retire into the fortress at the beginning of the night.

* When a place is intended to be assaulted by an Indian army, it is allowed to all those who are not upon duty, to go and risque their lives in attempting to enter the place, to share the plunder. Great numbers, both of cavalry and infantry, go on these expeditions; and though the hussars and dragoons have thirty rupees, or £. 3. 15 s. per month, many of them went in hopes to plunder Ayder's unfortunate subjects, who are afterwards indemnified by him.

The town of Caveripatnam is furrounded by an antique wall and rampart, with towers of hewn ftone: the Paler wafhes part of its walls; but this river, which is very broad, was not then more than a foot deep: the reft of the walls was defended by a dry ditch of no great depth.

About three o'clock, the different chiefs of the troops deftined for the attack having given notice that they were in readinefs, two falvos of the eight pieces of cannon ferved as a fignal; and on the fecond difcharge, from eighteen to twenty thoufand men iffued from all parts, with loud fhouts: fome began to crofs the river; others entered the ditch with wretched bamboo ladders; others again had only poles with hooks; and numbers had faftened hooks to their turban-cloths, which they threw on the ramparts, and attempted to fcramble up; and, laftly, another party were extremely bufy chopping the gates with hatchets: the whole fcene was very ftriking and laughable; and the activity of the affail-ants was vaftly increafed by the aftonifhment of the Englifh, who made no refiftance, but haftened hastened to the fortress, though not with celerity enough to save fifty Seapoys, an Indian captain, and an European serjeant, who were cut off in their retreat: these were instantly stripped, as were also the inhabitants, who were but few in number, the more opulent having retired before the English besieged the place.

It was not without difficulty that the town was cleared of these pillagers, who were slain in the houses and streets by the cannon of the fortress.

In the night after the attack a battery of twenty pieces of cannon, of eighteen and twenty-four pounds, was constructed, which announced itself at six in the morning by a full discharge, all the embrasures being unmasked at once. The construction of this battery was facilitated by a wall of earth belonging to a large house on an elevated ground, which the English had left standing after burning its roof. It is to be observed, that there is no trouble, in Ayder's army, to make platforms of wood for the batteries; the earth is sufficiently solid, and nothing is to be feared from

rain

rain during the fine feafon: the pieces are always mounted on their carriages, and confequently ready to be placed in battery; the carriages are very folid, and the fellies of the wheels very broad, fo that they do not cut into the earth. It muft likewife be owned, that in fieges of no great confequence, as well to fatisfy the impatience of Ayder as to quiet the murmurs of the gunners, and deceive the enemy, the pioneers often give the earth an appearance only of folidity: but, what will appear moft aftonifhing, and perhaps incredible, is, that the battery was partly conftructed with the fame gabions employed in the battery made ufe of by General Smith, which was ftill in good condition, and ready to have mounted cannon, if it had not been judged proper to place another to better advantage. The Englifh commandant had raifed two cavaliers of earth upon the baftions that fired on the battery, from whence he plunged with four fmall pieces of cannon, which killed and wounded many men, exclufive of thofe who fuffered from the mufquetry; the battery not being more than feventy paces from the body

body of the place: but the officer of Ayder, who conducted the attack, recollecting that the ancient Flibustiers took places without any other fire-arms than their buccaneers, which are long musquets of a large caliber, caused about two hundred of them, with their guns, to place themselves in proper positions behind some ruins. We have already observed that they are excellent markfmen; and their fire was so well directed, that in less than an hour it silenced that of the ramparts and cavaliers: ten or twelve cannoniers and a number of Seapoys were killed the first discharge; so that in a short time it became impossible for their officers to compel them to appear on the rampart: every discharge of a great gun from the place cost at least a cannonier, who was either killed or rendered incapable of fighting. It was this destructive fire that *, according to the account of the English, compelled them to hoist the white flag at nine in the morning, after three hours cannonade at most, without any breach, except a few stones

* This is exactly conformable to the account given by the English themselves.

that began to be loosened. Ayder was so surprised that he could not persuade himself of the truth of the fact, but went out of his tent to a rising ground to see the flag: bestowing a disgraceful appellation on the English, he ordered the commanding officer, who had waited on him for instructions concerning the capitulation, to refuse nothing that might be demanded.

In consequence of this, captain M..... obtained, that himself and his troops should march out with the honours of war: that the Europeans should retire to Madras by the way of Tripetour, Vailour, and Arcot: that the Seapoys should be at liberty to go where they pleased, or to enlist in the army of Ayder; which they almost all did, as well as the horsemen: that all the officers and soldiers should carry away what belonged to them; but that the arms, ammunition, stores, horses, and every thing belonging either to the king of England, the East India Company, or Mehemet Ali Khan, should be faithfully put into the hands of Ayder. Captain M..... observing the facility with which Ayder allowed

all

all his demands, was not afraid to ask payment for the provisions, which he said he had purchased with his own money, and was not sure of being repaid by the governor of Madras: this proposition was so much the more absurd, as all these provisions had been taken by force from the inhabitants of the country; which, however, did not prevent the English administration from paying him the value: besides which, as a recompence for his brave defence, the command of the garrison of Madras was bestowed on him. This facility of Ayder to suffer the English to enjoy the fruit * of their rapines, has apparently served greatly to facilitate the capture of places.

Ayder having caused the English garrison to evacuate the place, the day after the cap-

---

* It appears, that in the present war Ayder finds much more difficulty in taking places; which perhaps may arise from the artillery being neither so numerous nor so well served, or from the presence of General Coote, who, after the former war, was sent to India as commissary, and caused some officers to be punished. This cannot, however, be decided so far from the scene of action.

ture of Caveripatnam, marched his army the following day about two in the morning: at noon he pitched his camp on the banks of the Paler, where the camp remaining under the guard of the irregular troops, the army paſſed the river, and reſumed their march in ſeveral columns, with the cavalry at their head, followed by the grenadiers and artillery, the reſt of the infantry forming the rear.

The army marched in this order till ten at night, at which time they reſted about two hours in fields of carbi, a kind of pulſe that horſes and cattle are very deſirous of, and which they were ſuffered to eat at pleaſure. At midnight the moon roſe, and the army proceeded ; and at the break of day the huſſars and European dragoons joined the cavalry of Moɛtum, that was diſperſed in the woods at a ſmall diſtance from the Engliſh camp. This cavalry had been ſeven days in the open air, without tents or baggage, and Moɛtum fared like the reſt. It may be ſeen from this circumſtance, how far Ayder's troops are from being infeɛted with that want of hardineſs the Indians have been ſo continually

tinually reproached with. The five thousand grenadiers, as well as the artillery that followed the cavalry, arrived at the same time, having traverſed ſeventeen leagues in a march of twenty-eight hours, without taking more than four hours reſt: the fatigue theſe grenadiers had been ſubjected to, in the exerciſes and evolutions at their formation, had put them into a condition of making ſuch long and extraordinary marches. The reſt of the infantry remained in the fields of carbi, and did not begin their march till day-break.

It may, with juſtice, be a ſubject of admiration, that ſo numerous a train of artillery, drawn by oxen, could follow the troops with ſuch rapidity. This ſurpriſe will vaniſh, when it is known, that the oxen of India are very ſtrong; and that thoſe who are practiſed in drawing almoſt always go on a full trot: it is alſo known, how ſure-footed this animal is: the elephants aſſiſted in caſes of need, and a multitude of pioneers, that went before the artillery, made the roads practicable, and even eaſy.

General

General Smith, as we have already observed, supposed he might remain without molestation in his camp at Singueman, till the arrival of Colonel Wood; being persuaded that Caveripatnam would hold out at least as long against Ayder as it did against himself: but Ayder, who he believed to be at Caveripatnam, was already close upon him with his cavalry, his artillery, and his best infantry. Moctum had distributed his cavalry and Caleros with such judgment, that they possessed all the avenues to the English camp. It was Ayder's project, when the rest of his infantry should arrive, to convey his forces to a small plain between Singueman and Tirnmaly, and to take his post on the banks of a small river, of considerable depth, that General Smith would be under the necessity of passing in his way to Tirnmaly. By this position, Ayder would have prevented the junction of the two English armies, which must have thrown General Smith into the utmost embarrassment; because it would have subjected him to the necessity of taking the road through Tripetour, Arni, and

Arcot, and of traversing plains where he must have fought to disadvantage, on account of the numerous cavalry of his enemies.

But, contrary to expectation, Rocum Daulla arrived about ten in the morning, at the head of a large body of cavalry, announcing his arrival by the grand timbals, doubtless for the purpose of advising the English; besides which, after his junction with Ayder, he sent advice of the capture of Caveripatnam, and the arrival of the army in the environs of the camp. This is confirmed beyond contradiction by the manœuvre of the English, who raised their camp a little before noon. On the advice of this, Ayder mounted all his cavalry, and the infantry repaired to arms. The hussars and dragoons having orders to issue out of the wood, and shew themselves to the English army, found them in full march in a single column, coasting the river, and covering their baggages: their cavalry was at the head and rear of the column, and appeared desirous of gaining a hill that was before them.

The

The European commandant, who had been at the head of the European cavalry to reconnoitre the English, gave advice of what he had obferved, and of the apparent defigns of the enemy. Ayder, in confequence, gave orders to his grenadiers, fupported by his cavalry, to attack the English army; commanding the reft of his infantry likewife, who began to appear, to advance as quick as poffible.

To judge of the difadvantages under which Ayder's army fought, it will be fufficient to confider how much his infantry muft have been harraffed and fatigued by the prodigious march they had made without taking any repofe. This did not, however, prevent the grenadiers from marching with fuch order and firmnefs to the attack, as aftonifhed the English general.

The English army had gained the hill. It was compofed of three thoufand Europeans, ten thoufand Seapoys, and two thoufand horfe: all the infantry was in a fingle line, the English being in the centre; except fix hundred grenadiers or volunteers, feparated into two bodies, and closing the line with twenty-four pieces of cannon, that composed the whole of the English artillery. The artillery was placed in the centre and flanks of the line: every regiment had its own field-pieces. The cavalry, divided into two bodies, was at the front and rear of the baggage; it formed the two sides of a triangle, of which the infantry constituted the third; whose fire, as well as that of the artillery, would have flanked any cavalry that might have attacked them. The slope of the hill was gentle, but it was covered with underwood that impeded the march of those Indian battalions who approached to attack the English. Notwithstanding this obstacle, they advanced to the distance of twenty-five paces, and fought many hours without losing ground, in spite of the enemy's musquetry and cannon; giving the rest of the infantry time to come up, though not with the same courage and ardour as the grenadiers; except eight or nine hundred volunteers from the different corps, who, led on by the European serjeants, attacked the left of the English line, and took two pieces of cannon. But a body a body of English, immediately sent to assist, repulsed them, and recovered the cannon, a little before night; which alone put an end to the firing on both sides: the two armies resting on the field, as if intending to continue the action. The disadvantages under which Ayder's infantry fought in this battle, and the good conduct of his grenadiers, must appear surprising to Europeans, who are accustomed to entertain a bad opinion of the bravery of the Indians: it appeared so to General Smith, who speaks in high terms of them, as well as of the European officers that commanded them. But to say the truth, this infantry was sustained by sixty pieces of large cannon, pointed by able gunners, who made great ravages among the English infantry, that was uncovered from head to foot; while the English artillery did little injury to Ayder's infantry, on account of the difficulty of aiming well in pointing downwards. -This difference of advantage compensated, in some respect, for the advantage of position, and in the number of musquets, that were more than double those of the grenadiers,

diers, before they were joined by the rest of the infantry.

'In this battle Ayder lost nine hundred of his grenadiers; a loss so much the more considerable, as they were brave men, accustomed to fatigue, and who never gave way. The Bacsi, or minister of war, who has the right of marching at the head of the infantry, though he does not command them, was killed by a cannon-ball: and the cavalry, which was of no use in this day's service, nevertheless lost some men and horses, the English artillery having good play among so numerous a troop.

It was perceived, about eleven at night, that the English retired in silence. Ayder gave orders to his troops not to attempt to molest them, the cavalry not being able to attack the English infantry in the night; and he was desirous of giving some repose to his infantry, who had distinguished themselves, and had need of rest.

Before day-break, the cavalry, headed by the hussars and dragoons, set out in pursuit of the English army, who had abandoned their baggage

baggage for the sake of carrying off their wounded. General Smith himself set the example: the dragoons finding part of his kitchen utensils, and two valuable trunks belonging to Major Bonjour, a Genevan officer, esteemed by the English, and who did the duty of major-general of their army,—these baggages afforded the hussars and dragoons excellent plunder. In order more effectually to secure a conveyance for their wounded, the English threw their ammunition and stores into the river, from whence the Indians recovered the balls and sacks of rice; and, in order to conceal their loss, they buried their dead: but the night, and their haste, caused them to perform this duty with so little care, that the bodies were many of them partly uncovered. The avidity of the soldiers for plunder, when it is permitted, induced them to dig up the dead, in order to get the clothes they were wrapped in.

In spite of the haste employed by Ayder's cavalry in pursuit of the English, they gained Tirnmaly, with no other loss than two small iron three-pounders they themselves left behind

hind; and there was only one skirmish in sight of Tirnmaly, between the grenadiers, who formed the rear-guard of the English, and the hussars and dragoons, one of whom only was wounded. Thus it was that General Smith escaped the risque he would have run, if Ayder, with his army, could have taken his post beyond the river, as he had projected.

All the irregular troops had been left in the camp at Paler; because this kind of troops being without discipline, it would have been difficult to have kept them out of sight of the English; and because the enemy's spies are generally of this body of troops.

Ayder, elated with the glory of having caused the English to fly before him, advanced, and encamped a league and a half from Tirnmaly, in a place full of large rocks, and separated from Tirnmaly by a plain; and, as he was encamped very near the enemy, to whose method of beating the Indians by attacks in the night he was no stranger, he took every precaution that could be required to secure his camp from any surprize.

A large

A large opening between thefe rocks, that might have been taken for a work of art, and behind which his camp was fituated, was fortified by a redoubt. All the heights were occupied by guards, whofe centinels continually called *Cabordor!* which fignifies *Take care of yourfelf!* Guards of cavalry and Caleros were difpatched clofe to Tirnmaly, with rockets to make fignals; fo that the Englifh could make no movement to attack the camp of Ayder, without his being immediately advifed. But General Smith had no intention to run any rifque till Colonel Wood fhould join him with his army, which had been augmented, and was eight or nine thoufand ftrong, exclufive of a body of Caleros from Tanjaor.

Ayder, who ought to have fent a ftrong detachment, or the whole of his army, to prevent this junction, fuffered it to take place, in fpite of all the advice that was given him on the fubject. He continued to keep his army collected, and to make war in a country where his cavalry was almoft entirely ufelefs; efpecially while General Smith remained in his camp at Tirnmaly,

maly, situated between two mountains on which there are fortresses; having his van covered by the town, and a tank, where no force could arrive but through narrow passes, defended by retrenchments with artillery.

His hope was to draw his enemy out of their camp. For this purpose he caused his infantry to make a kind of parade every day; sometimes coming within reach of the artillery with all his troops, and at other times with his infantry alone. He lost his time so effectually, that Colonel Wood joined his forces to those of General Smith.

Notwithstanding this junction, which made the English army amount to above five-and-twenty thousand good troops, four thousand five hundred being Europeans, General Smith did not think proper to expose himself in the plain against Ayder; but, to give him an opportunity of attacking him in a country the most favourable to his infantry, he quitted his camp at Tirnmaly, and marching to the left at day break, he pitched *another camp two leagues from Tirnmaly, that his army might be less confined.*

Ayder,

Ayder, informed of the design of the English general, was desirous of laying a snare for him, that he communicated to no one, and which might have been attended with fatal consequences. The fact is this: The English army had to pass through a plain, bounded on all sides by woods and small eminences: Ayder gave orders, in the evening, to the chiefs of his artillery and infantry, to march into this plain at the dawn of day; entering it by a kind of valley that enlarged itself into the flat ground. He himself, in consequence of his project, departed at two in the morning with all his cavalry, which, by a very large circuit, he conducted into the close places that bordered the plain. They who commanded his infantry being apprized of his departure, began their march at the appointed hour; not doubting but that they should either find the cavalry at the plain, or receive orders relative to their disposition. They were highly astonished, on their arrival, not to see a single horseman, nor any other troops whatsoever. In proportion as the entrance grew larger, the infantry extended their front, and drew themselves into order

order of battle. The plain, though to appearance even, was divided in two by a rising ground. Some officers, who went before, were astonished, on mounting the eminence, to find the English army drawn up in order of battle behind it. As there had been no orders given for attacking them, and no news had arrived of Ayder and his cavalry, a council, held hastily on the spot, decided that they should retire to the entrance of the valley, in order to post themselves more advantageously; while scouts were dispatched on all sides to obtain news, and the orders of the Nabob.

The English, who had been advised of the ambuscade prepared for them by Ayder, remained in order of battle till the beginning of the night, when they entered their new camp. The infantry and artillery of Ayder returned to theirs; and the prince returned very late in the night with his cavalry, much fatigued with having rode ten leagues in very bad ground, and without having taken any nourishment. Ayder supposed that General Smith was ignorant of the march of his cavalry; and would have been tempted to attack his

his infantry, who apparently were not supported by any horse: by which means he expected to find an opportunity of falling upon the English army with his horse. We may easily imagine that things would have been conducted in another manner, if he had communicated his project.

As Tipou Saeb, who was then about seventeen years of age, is now the right hand of his father, and is the person who has had the most brilliant success against the English,—we think it proper to mention his conduct on this occasion. Ayder, who passionately loves his son, and is acquainted with his zeal and courage, was fearful respecting him on account of his very early age: for this reason, he usually entrusted him with the guard of the camp, when he supposed the day would prove too fatiguing or dangerous. The young prince, being charged with the care of the camp on the present occasion, was in great pain when the infantry returned, and the night closed in, without any news concerning his father and the cavalry. Two hours after dark, that is to say about eight o'clock, he sent for all the generals,

generals, gave them a short account of the state of affairs, and demanded their advice. The unanimous opinion was, that the English were too weak in cavalry to make any attempt against the Nabob; and that they could not come to attack the camp but by marching three leagues, and passing through straits where guards were placed. The prince replied to them, " As I have no orders from my father, I have need of your experience to direct my actions: I will wait here with patience and confidence according to your advice; and am much obliged to you for your attention and care." The whole company had not yet left the prince, when word was brought that Moctum, his uncle, second commander of the army, had entered the camp, having taken the van-guard with some horse.

Ayder, always indefatigable, advanced at dawn towards Tirnmaly, with four thousand infantry and twenty pieces of cannon. The town was open to him; but while he was making the proper disposition to attack the fortresses, he learned that General Smith was in motion to attack him. This intelligence obliged

obliged him to return into his camp; not chufing to fight in a pofition where his cavalry would have been of no fervice to him.

He removed his camp the next day, becaufe he could not reach that of the Englifh but by narrow paffes, or by marching above ten leagues; though the camps were not above four leagues afunder. After paffing by the rear of Nizam Daulla's army, that had arrived two days before, and was encamped in a fine plain, he pitched his camp to the left hand of Nizam, but in advance, being then about four leagues from the Englifh, with a plain before him, interfperfed with fome wood and a pond that covered the left of the Englifh camp.

The very evening that Ayder had changed his camp, the Englifh at the clofe of day ftruck their tents; the news of which was quickly carried to Ayder, and obliged him to keep his men to their arms all night. But the Englifh contented themfelves to pafs the night in the open air; and at fun-rife they again fet up their tents. This manœuvre was repeated, for no pofitive reafon that can be deduced, the four following nights, in fpite of the frequent

showers

showers they were expofed to; and Ayder, in confequence, fortified his camp with four large redoubts.

As the Englifh camp was always furrounded with cavalry and light troops, as well on foot as on horfeback, who had taken poffeffion of all the paffages, they could not receive provifion and ammunition except from Tirnmaly, where they had no other ftores than rice. Their troops therefore fuffered much, as Ayder was well inftructed by the capture of patmars or couriers paffing between the army and Madras, and likewife by the reports of individuals. The governor of Madras blamed Geneneral Smith for having given the foldiers their rations of arrack in money; faying that money, being fcarce, ought to be fparingly diftributed, and that it would have been fufficient to have promifed the men their due from the council of Madras. In a letter to the paymafter, he blamed him for having refufed to pay the troops their money in lieu of arrack, at the orders of the general; obferving, that no one in the army can refufe obedience to the general, who is alone refponfible for the

confeconsequences of his orders and dispositions. The governor likewise wrote to the doctor, who was commissary to the army, to continue to instruct him of all that passed, &c.

This knowledge of the inconvenience sustained by the English ought to have determined Ayder to continue the plan of investing the army, and ravaging the country. The English, impatient, no doubt, and desirous of extricating themselves out of their disagreeable situation, either by a night attack or by removing their camp, began to march about ten at night, after having struck their tents as usual. Ayder was soon informed of this unexpected march, by the repeated signals of rockets; and a short time after was apprized that their course was directed to the camp of Nizam Daulla.

The news was extremely embarrassing to the Nabob. He had the best founded suspicions of a secret correspondence between Rocum Daulla and the English, and had sufficient reason to believe that Nizam himself had not the best intentions towards him. If Nizam was in concert with the English, his army, which was without defence on the side of his ally, was very much exposed to danger; and on the other hand, without considering the probability of actual treachery, if the English should attack Nizam, the little order that prevailed in his army might be dangerous to his own, where the fugitives would not fail to fly for shelter and protection. Having called a council in a small casemate where Ayder usually slept, at the head of his camp, it was resolved, that his army should be in readiness to march and intercept the English in their course to Nizam's army; which it was easy to do, as they had no more than a league and half of ground to pass, whereas the English had near six: and that, in the mean time, the European commandant should march with all the irregular troops, and those dispersed in the country, to reach the front of the English army; and, by harrassing them, retard their march, so that they might not be able to reach Nizam's army before day-light.

It was about one in the morning when this officer learned that the English army was advanced about three leagues on their way.

He

He immediately assembled the greater part of the chiefs of the Caleros and Carnates, and commanded them to approach as near the English army as they could; extending themselves on their flank the whole length of the line, without fear of spreading themselves too much, and not to fire till within fifteen paces; —that they might fire at pleasure, though as quickly as possible, taking care every man to lie flat on the ground after making his discharge. This last piece of advice might have been spared; but it had its weight with them, as it was a tacit approbation of their manner of fighting. They very exactly obeyed their orders; their approach, and the great extent of ground they covered, which was known to the English by the matches of their musquets, stopped the march of the English, and obliged them to call into the column the small detached parties that were on their flank, no doubt for fear they should be surrounded. The fire of the Caleros having commenced, the English, who ought to have despised them, faced about and answered by platoons, which made much noise, and did little mischief for the space of more than two hours, the Caleros returning their fire to the best of their abilities. An hour and half before day-break, the English marched to their left, and pitched another camp that was nearer Tirnmaly, which covered their right; the bank of a large pond was on their left, and before them a mountain of considerable height (where they placed a battalion of Seapoys) and surrounded with rocks and underwood, impracticable for cavalry.

After reconnoitring the English camp, Ayder raised his own, and took another station, that was within two leagues of theirs, and so situated as to prevent the enemy from attacking the army of Nizam, without first engaging his own.

By the new position of both armies, the numerous cavalry of the two Subas became still more useless and difficult to be supported; which induced Ayder to attend to a piece of advice that had long been given him,—to send a large detachment from his army to take Godelour, an English factory two leagues from Pondicherry; and to return by following

ing the sea coast as far as Madras, whose environs they were to ravage and lay waste: a step that could not fail in obliging the council to recal the army for their own defence, which would have produced the greatest discredit and real prejudice to the Company's affairs.

This detachment was on the point of departing, commanded by the European officer who gave the advice, and was assured of taking Godelour, from his intimate acquaintance with the place: but an English emissary, introduced into the camp of Ayder, and who had acquired the confidence of Raza Saeb, ancient Nabob of Arcot, a man of a contracted understanding, and much given to suspicion and jealousy, took the advantage, by means of this man, to make Ayder believe, that the whole was no more than a contrivance of the French officer to return to Pondicherry with his troop, being recalled (as it was insidiously affirmed) by the governor of that place.

If the answer of the governor of Pondicherry to the letters of the two Nabobs had been

been less precise, and had given some hope of assistance to them, as sound policy perhaps required, the imposture of the English emissary would have made no impression on the mind of Ayder; and the commerce of Pondicherry would, by the ruin of Godelour, have been benefited by the loss of commerce the English would have sustained.

Ayder had so much regard for the French officer who was to have commanded the expedition against Godelour, that he had caused Nizam Daulla, the Suba of Decan, to grant him a Zaghire, or immediate fief of the empire, without any vassalship to the Nabob of Arcot, all the country along the coast between the rivers of Alemparvy and Divicoty, and a line drawn from one river to the other, touching and including Paniroti. The Paravana or patent recited, that this gift was made in return for the great services rendered to the empire by the said officer; and that it was without any other obligation than that of maintaining two hundred Europeans for the guard of the country, whose revenue was estimated at eight lacks of rupees; with a promise promife of enlargement of the territory, if it should prove lefs. Ayder, and his fon, as Nabob of Arcot, had confirmed and ratified this donation.

The French officer, who was firmly perfuaded that the Englifh and Mehemet Ali Khan would lofe all the Nabobfhip of Arcot in this war, thought it expedient to profit by the favour of Ayder, by obtaining a gift that would be fo ufeful to his country. He did not wait till conqueft had put that Nabob in poffeffion of the territory; prefuming, perhaps with reafon, that he might not then be fo generous. The inveftiture, which ought to have been a fecret in the cabinet, was made public by the fecretaries of Rocum Daulla, Divan and keeper of the great feal, who came in ceremony to compliment the officer, and receive his prefent on the occafion. This gift excited the jealoufy of Raza Saeb and fome others, and was doubtlefs one of the inducements that led Ayder to fufpect the French officer.

But, whatever may have been the caufe, there is no doubt that Ayder was fearful of suffering his Europeans to approach too near Pondicherry. He therefore informed the French officer, that, as he could not then spare any infantry, it would be proper to defer the capture of Godelour till another opportunity; but that he would dispatch a body of cavalry to destroy the country close up to the gates of Madras; "and as it is no more than a kind of course," said he, "and my son has never yet had any command, it will be doing him a great pleasure to give him charge of this operation, at the head of five thousand horse." It may, perhaps, seem surprising that Ayder should use so much address to make this officer acquiesce with a good grace in the substituting another general to the command of a detachment that had been promised him; but no prince can possess to greater advantage the art of softening his refusal; so that he never appears to deny any thing. In consequence of this conference, the young prince departed with his detachment; and advanced with so much speed and secrecy towards Madras, that the governor, Mehemet Ali Khan and his son, together with Colonel Call, and almost all

the

the council, very narrowly efcaped being taken in the country-houfe at the Company's garden. Happily for them a fmall veffel, that by accident was oppofite the garden, furnifhed them with the means of efcaping, which otherwife would have been impoffible. Their flight was fo precipitate, that the governor did not ftay for his hat and fword, which were taken by the foldiery, as well as the breakfaft equipage; it being the cuftom at Madras to take the air every morning, and breakfaft in the country. The governor and his company would infallibly have been made prifoners, if a domeftic of their French emiffary in Ayder's camp, fent exprefsly to apprize them of the incurfion, had not arrived the very moment they were preparing to take their ufual ride. The cavalry of Ayder arrived full fpeed, and cut off their return to Madras: Mehemet Ali Khan, who alone took the high road, efcaped being taken only by the goodnefs of his horfe. If the governor had had the misfortune to have been taken, his own vanity and prefumption would have been the caufe: for his company had fcarcely met, before a crowd

crowd of the country people ran past towards Fort St. George, crying *Maratta! Maratta!* the people of the coast never having, before the present war, experienced any incursions except from that nation. The governor and other English, instead of paying any attention to the cries of the fugitives, were much diverted with the circumstance. A second troop passing by, and some of the company observing that the business deserved attention, the governor answered, " The enemy's cavalry cannot arrive here without first passing by fortresses where we have garrisons, whose commandants would send me advice: the terror of these people is certainly a panic; and to put an end to it, I will order the Chaubuc * to the next that come to alarm us in this manner." Every body applauded his discourse, according to the established custom

---

* The Chaubuc is a long strap of leather at the end of a stick, with which the Indians are chastised without much ceremony. The governor and counsellors of Madras have always Chaubuckers before their palanquins, ready to exercise this act of justice, if it deserves the name.

of

of crying *Amen* to what is said by men in power. But in the instant arrived a crowd from St. Thomas\*, many of whom were wounded; they announced that the enemy were plundering that town. The whole company was seized with fear, and had just time

---

\* The town of St. Thomas is supposed to belong to the Portuguese, and the colours of that nation are still displayed at the place. The bishop takes the title of governor. It is entirely open, and the English do not scruple to keep Seapoys in garrison there. The governor of Madras often sends for the bishop, as if he were at his orders; and his house and church are occasionally searched, without any respect of places. Having received orders from his court to expel the Jesuits, they have remained in their convent, under the protection of the English, preserving their habit, and exercising their functions, in spite of the interdiction. This poor bishop is so much the slave of the English, that, notwithstanding the ill treatment he receives, they compel him to give a Portuguese passport to an English vessel that trades every year from Madras to the Manillas, where it is received by virtue of the false passport of the Portuguese governor, who is acknowledged by the English merely for their own convenience.

to save themselves by the sea-coast, in consequence of the advice so luckily given them.

While Tipou Saeb ravaged the environs of Madras, his father reconnoitred the English camp; which it was easy for him to do, without danger, from a plain on the top of a hill that commanded a view of the rocks and underwood we have described. The Nabob perceived that he could annoy a part of their camp with large cannon; and having taken his resolution, he caused his army to march the next day early, and conveying some large pieces of cannon to the top of the hill, he caused them to be pointed at the English camp, where they carried admirably well, and occasioned a kind of disorder and haste in striking and removing tents, &c. Ayder, delighted at having thus insulted the English, caused all his artillery, even the very smallest pieces, to be drawn up the hill for the purpose of making a vain parade, though the greater part of the balls could never reach the English: he imagined he should give the enemy a high idea of his forces, and intimidate them by shewing them all this artillery, and the vivacity

vacity and spirit it was worked with; and, in order that his intention might be answered, he encouraged the soldiers himself, by giving money to the cannoniers of those pieces that appeared to be best served:—all which was matter of derision and laughter to the English; and in reality answered no other purpose, than that of frightening the feathered inhabitants of the underwood that grew on the hill-side.

While Ayder thus exercised his artillery, and kept his infantry in parade, his cavalry gallopped about the plain to almost as little effect as the discharge of the greatest part of his artillery. Nizam, who did not think proper on this occasion to be an idle spectator, had marched with his army, nearly at the same time as his ally, and caused his cavalry to parade round the English camp: but about three in the afternoon, with his whole infantry, he attacked the Seapoys that General Smith had posted on the mountain. To defend themselves against this attack, the Seapoys were obliged to take positions that exposed them to the artillery of Ayder: seeing themselves obliged to give way, they
made

made several signals to General Smith, who marched to their assistance with his whole army. It was near four in the evening, when his columns were observed to march out. Ayder immediately caused his artillery and infantry to descend from the hill, and recalled his cavalry, in order to face the English with his whole force. His troops were scarcely drawn up, in order to march, before the whole infantry of Nizam was seen in the most precipitate flight and disorder; while his cavalry appeared to advance bravely and in good order against the English, followed by his artillery: but instead of extending itself in the plain, to the left of Ayder, the troop placed itself between the English and his army, so as entirely to mask it from their sight. The English advanced along the banks of the pond near the mountain, marching on ground covered with stones and shrubs \*,
whose

---

\* The shrub that grows in all this part of India, and in all the uncultivated lands, is of the greatest utility. Its wood, leaves, and flower, distil a kind of syrup, which the great heat, I imagine, prevents
from

whose branches being very flexible, are no great inconvenience for infantry. They were formed into two columns, having their cavalry in their rear, and their artillery in front, which firing on the cavalry, caused them to give way, and in a short time put them to flight full speed by the shortest way, which happened to be through the camp of Ayder, across which they drove, spreading terror and disorder as they went. Ayder perceiving the flight of Nizam and all his army, found himself exceedingly embarrassed, as he had every reason to suspect some treachery: he was likewise apprehensive, that, while he fought with the English, his camp would be plundered by the fugitives: and the approach of night added to the trouble that employed his thoughts.

When the dispersion of Nizam's army had left the English army uncovered, it was seen

---

from forming into lumps, like honey. It is with this shrub that the distillers, who follow the Indian camps, make their arrack, by adding more or less sugar, according to the season.

advancing in one full line, with the cavalry in reserve. The artillery of Ayder, distributed along the front of his infantry, made a few discharges, which must have slain a number of the enemy; but as the ridiculous cannonade from the top of the hill had exhausted his ammunition, his great guns soon became useless to him: the cavalry that formed the two wings having received orders to charge, the right wing, where the hussars and dragoons were, made several charges, and advanced within pistol-shot; but could never stand against the fire of the English artillery and musquetry. The left wing, for some unknown reason, made only one charge, and afterwards kept at a sufficient distance from the fire. Ayder seeing very little hope of beating the English, who had the advantage of artillery, and the night closing in being in favour of their infantry, yielded the field of battle, and retreated in good order; the Nabob himself forming the rear-guard at the head of his cavalry. He withdrew his army into their camp, without leaving the English any mark of their victory, except one of the iron three-

three-pounders they themselves had loft before, whose oxen were killed, and might have been easily replaced by the oxen from the empty ammunition waggons, if Ayder would have consented. The English made no prisoners, except a Portuguese officer of the Topasses, who, being wounded, was given to be carried by four of his soldiers, and thrown by them into a ditch; and a Pandari, who was likewise wounded: all the other wounded were brought off. The number of killed in the army of the two Subas, did not exceed four hundred men. The English followed Ayder to his camp; but his situation between two mountains, a large pond, and two redoubts, between which they must have passed, prevented them from thinking of the attack. They contented themselves with firing some cannon across the pond, none of which reached the camp; and passed the night in the open air, a good cannon shot distant from the redoubts.

Upon the arrival of Ayder in his camp, he found it in confusion; the greater part of the servants and other people in the suite of the army,

army, terrified at the flight of Nizam and his troops, having ran off, leaving the camp all standing. After placing his infantry in the redoubts, and behind a retrenchment hastily thrown up, he ordered all his heavy artillery and baggage to march: the execution of this order was attended with great difficulty. Ayder has a particular talent in chusing places where his camp can be in security, as well from the nature of the ground, as from the defences that art can add; in which particular he has gained the praises of General Smith, who himself possesses this talent in a superior degree. The continual wars of Ayder with the Marattas, who are far superior to him in cavalry, have no doubt obliged him to make a particular study of the art of encamping in advantageous positions, which are without number in his dominions; all the country being intersected by mountains and vallies, and covered with towns, fortresses, ponds, and woods. But he has the fault of not projecting easy sorties to his camps; though the inconveniencies have been often represented to him, especially on the

occasion

occasion of the retreat after the battle of Tirnmaly; his camp having no other way out behind, but by a pass filled with rocks and underwood, through which was a winding, narrow road, scarcely practicable for a single carriage. This road was very soon choaked up by the number of beasts of burthen, whose owners had anticipated the order for raising the camp. The pass was divided into two, one leading to the camp of Nizam: all the baggage marched at their own discretion; a considerable number took the right hand road, and crossed the immense baggages of Nizam's army, that marched in the greatest disorder, intermixed with artillery. The consequence of all this disorder was, a stoppage, that prevented the march of Ayder's artillery, in spite of all the pains that were taken to get forward by the light of more than a hundred torches*; for, as they com-

* These torches must appear very extraordinary in Europe, on account of the many risques they must be productive of: but the Indians have not yet been induced to submit to reason, with regard to their imprudent use of torches and fires.

pelled the loaded beasts to walk on the borders of the road, they fell and overthrew their burthens; which occasioned cries and a dreadful tumult, the noise being repeated by the mountains: so that nothing better could be done, than to dispatch some troops to stop the march, and give orders for every one to remain where he was till morning. When the day appeared, regularity was soon restored, as Nizam's army was already in the plain. If General Smith had detached a small party of his infantry, by a circuit of two leagues, they might have entered the camp of Nizam; and by a few shot among the fugitives and conductors of baggage, they might have occasioned so much disorder, as would have rendered the consequences of the victory of the greatest importance: for, though he met with no molestation after his defeat, he left seven or eight pieces of large cannon in his camp \*: Ayder caused the

---

\* The English have published, that they took many pieces of cannon belonging to Nizam on the day

the carriages to be repaired, and sent them to him with the harness. Even the silver plate, and other valuable effects of Nizam, were found in the roads.

Ayder, instead of imitating the cowardice of Nizam, appeared at day-break, with his troops drawn up in order of battle, at the entrance of his camp: all his infantry being in the first line, and part of his cavalry in the second. In this position he made the English respect him. When his artillery and baggage had gained the plain, he retired with his army, himself forming the rear-guard with his grenadiers, who did not quit that post of honour to the cavalry, till after the whole army had reached the plain. The English, who followed them, durst not make any attack, but fired a few cannon, which

day of battle, which they afterwards returned when they made an accommodation with them. There are strong reasons for doubting this fact; because these pieces were not conducted in triumph to Madras, where they would have been exhibited, if it were for no other reason than because they were ornamented with fleurs de lis.

flew four men, including a quarter-master of dragoons, who was struck by the last rebound of a ball *.

It will readily be supposed, that General Smith hastened to forward the news of this victory to Madras, which extricated the government of that settlement out of the most tormenting embarrassment. The unexpected incursion of Ayder's son had thrown them into the greatest consternation: the garrison of Fort St. George consisted only of two hundred Europeans, and six hundred Seapoys; so that the Black Town, which is properly the town of Madras, was at the discretion of Tippou Saeb, a youth of eighteen. This town contains a great number of inhabitants, not less than four hundred thousand, according to the English valuation; and their num-

---

* The contrast of Ayder's army with that of Nizam, both in the battle and retreat, may serve to shew what kind of armies those were that were beat by a small number of Europeans; and likewise what the English and other Europeans, who flatter themselves with conquests in India, may expect in future.

ber was then vaſtly augmented by the fugitives from the country. Though it bears the name of the Black Town, it is inhabited by great numbers of Europeans of all nations, who have warehouſes furniſhed with the richeſt products of every country. Among others, there is a large colony of very rich Armenians, poſſeſſed of immenſe riches; and great numbers of Guzerats, or wealthy bankers, dealers in pearls, precious ſtones, and coral: in ſhort, this town is always one of the richeſt emporiums in the world, and was then defended only by a wall of earth breaſt-high, and entirely without any troops whatever.

The terror that ſpread itſelf among this immenſe people, when they ſaw the fugitives from the country enter, was ſo great, that they imagined the whole army of Ayder, headed by himſelf in perſon, was on the point of entering the town. Men, women, and children all ran to take refuge in Fort St. George, abandoning their houſes and all they poſſeſſed. As the governor, counſellors, commandant, &c. were not yet arrived, no one gave orders to ſhut the gates; ſo that in a short time the fort was crowded with a multitude of people, that filled the streets, the ditches, and even covered the glacis. The governor, on his arrival, could with difficulty force a passage to his house; where he entirely lost all fortitude, and remained two days with his head resting on a table, suffering Colonel Call, the chief engineer, and a man of abilities, to take the charge of every thing. This gentleman did his utmost; but has since confessed, that if Ayder's son had entered the Black Town, and pursued the fugitives, nothing could have prevented his taking Fort St. George. But this young prince was without experience; and his cavalry having approached the Black Town by the road from St. Thomas, passed of necessity under the cannon of the fort, a few discharges of which served to impose on him. Tippou Saeb convened a council, where the advice of the grand almoner\*, who had been sent with him in

---

\* This grand almoner was the friend of Ayder.— He will be mentioned in the portraits of the great men,

in quality of Mentor, was, that it was not proper to run the rifque of entering the Black Town: but that the orders of Ayder ought ftrictly to be followed, namely, to ravage the environs of Madras: and more particularly, not to hazard the life of the prince by expofing him to the cannon of Fort St. George, or any other fortrefs. Every one was obliged to fubmit to this opinion, which, it may be affirmed, was the caufe of faving the Englifh, and other inhabitants of Madras, the fum of more than one hundred millions of French money, that might have been loft to them by burning the Black Town, or forcing the governor and council to accept of peace on the hardeft terms, by threatening them with this confequence.

The Author of thefe Memoirs had advifed Ayder to befiege and take the Black Town of Madras, and to burn it; though he did not

men, and efpecially the friends and confidents of Ayder. Nothing can ferve more effectually to difplay the true character of a prince, than accurate portraits of the people that enjoy his favour.

imagine

imagine the thing to be so easy; yet his advice was partly the cause why he did not accompany the young prince, for fear of exposing him; and it is this advice alone that was the ground of the persecutions of Governor B.... against him, as well as the foundation of a legal process, in which no other evidence was brought than that of the English spies, who affirmed that they heard him give it. But this proceeding, contrary to every notion of justice and the laws of nations, was an ordinary act of that despotism the English have arrogated and exercised in India.

Though the town of Madras suffered no damage, because Colonel Call, having armed all the Europeans he could collect, dispatched some Seapoys and volunteers to defend the entrance of the Black Town, who prevented the pillagers from approaching; yet the damage sustained by the English was, nevertheless, very considerable. They have superb houses in the neighbourhood of Madras, richly furnished: and all the villages, which are very numerous and full of people, are inhabited by painters and manufacturers of every kind, who
were

were all pillaged, or affirmed they were in order to take advantage of not restoring the works that were entrusted in their hands, or paid for in advance. An English merchant, named *Debonnaire*, of French extraction, was the only one of the inhabitants of Madras who did not suffer by the ravages made by Ayder's troops round that city: not by way of gratitude for the services he had done Maffous Khan, the friend of Ayder; but by the effect of chance, which led Caki Saib, grand almoner of Ayder, and his real friend, to fix his residence in the country house of this merchant, which was situated at St. Thomas's Mount, a league and half from Madras. On the appearance of Ayder's cavalry seen from the mount, the servants of Mr. Debonnaire made their escape, with his children; leaving all the moveables and effects to the mercy of the enemy. The situation of the house was agreeable to Caki Saib, who chose it for his residence during the time Tippou Saeb remained in the environs of Madras. On his entering the house, he told the gardeners that he was a man of peace, and that his presence would secure

secure the house from insult. He forbade his people either to take or spoil the smallest thing; and having assured himself that his orders were not infringed, he enquired the name of the proprietor, and sent one of his gardeners, accompanied by one of his own people, to carry him his children's clothes, with fruits and herbs; assuring him that nothing in his house should be either damaged or stolen, but that he himself would overlook the gardeners, and see they did their duty; and would take care to send him the necessary produce of his garden every day, which he punctually performed. The young prince, in a visit to the grand almoner, was desirous of taking a microscope; but that nobleman would not consent, but wrote to Mr. Debonnaire to set a price upon the instrument; and it was not till he had received the merchant's second letter, that he consented to offer it as a present, on his part, to the son of Ayder.

The fugitives from the environs of Madras having spread themselves all over the coast, carried the news of the capture of that town by Ayder Ali Khan; and it came to Europe by by the way of Pondicherry, Tranquebar, and the other European settlements. The caravans, and every possible conveyance, distributed this news with pleasure; for the jealousy and hatred that other nations have conceived against the English, smothered the account they themselves had given of their victory at Tirnmaly. The consequence was, that the price of the Company's stock, at London, fell at once from 275 to 222. General Smith, to convey the news of his victory with readiness and expedition to Madras, dispatched a courier mounted on a dromedary, who, instead of avoiding the troops of Ayder, addressed himself to them, to demand news of the Schazade, or king's son, saying, that he was charged by his father to inform him of the loss of the battle at Tirnmaly, and to order him to rejoin him. By means of this stratagem he succeeded in gaining access to the town of Madras, though the son of Ayder was not above half a league distant. The governor, on receipt of General Smith's letters, announced the victory to the people by one hundred and one guns; and distributed the

the moſt exaggerated accounts of the advantages gained over Ayder.

The young prince, aſtoniſhed at ſo unexpected an event, conſulted his council, who unanimouſly adviſed him to rejoin the armies of the Subas as early as poſſible; which he executed in good order, carrying with him four monks, and a prieſt, grand vicar of the biſhop of St. Thomas, who was then at Pondicherry. On the reputation of Ayder's lenity, theſe prieſts did not think proper to follow the example of the other inhabitants of St. Thomas, by abandoning their habitations. But as Ayder had recommended to his ſon to bring away ſome perſon of diſtinction, who might inſtruct him concerning the forces of the Engliſh, and the ſuccours they expected from Europe or elſewhere,—for want of more important perſonages, he engaged theſe monks to accompany him; and conducted them with all poſſible care and attention, though by a diſagreeable carriage; having cauſed them to mount two and two on the backs of camels, a beaſt whoſe pace is very fatiguing. Their journey

journey having lasted five days, they arrived worn out with fatigue, and in the most deplorable condition; especially the Jesuits, who wore their square bonnets, and who, to retain this head-dress, and at the same time to defend themselves from the heat of the sun, had been under the necessity of wrapping their heads in painted silks given them for that purpose.

The battle of Tirnmaly happening in the month of November, which is in the rainy season in that part of India where the theatre of war then was, General Smith thought proper to send his army to quarters, as they had already suffered greatly. He distributed it into Vailour, Arcot, Cangivaromarni, Gingi, &c. after having strongly garrisoned Tirnmaly, Vaniambari, Ambour, and other advanced places.

The loss of the battle of Tirnmaly, though of so little importance, spread itself over all Indostan with the greatest rapidity; and was variously related, according to the dispositions of the narrators. Ayder was very little concerned at an event that he attributed solely
to

to the fault of Nizam; whose alliance, instead of producing advantage, was a real burthen to him. Nizam, on his side, perceiving that the conquest of the country of Arcot was by no means so near a conclusion as he had flattered himself, was desirous of returning to his own dominions; but he was desirous first of extorting money from Ayder, as well as from the English and Mehemet Ali Khan. The different motives and intentions of the two Subas augmented the distrust that was between them; but, instead of its becoming apparent, they were both careful to redouble the public testimonials of mutual friendship. Nizam Daulla, on the return of Tippou Saeb, invited Ayder, and all the great men of his court, to a superb festival. He rendered the highest honours to that sovereign; and, among other things, caused him to sit on a kind of throne or sopha of massy gold, with cushions of cloth of gold, which he presented him with in the evening, when they parted. He likewise gave a name of honour to Tippou Saeb, relative to his expedition against Madras; and bestowed honourable titles

tles on several of the retinue \*, who were most in Ayder's favour. A few days after, Nizam was invited by Ayder in his turn; but, instead of causing him to sit on a throne of wrought gold, a sopha was prepared with sacks of pagodas and gold rupees, covered with fine carpets, and cushions of velvet, with a gold ground; all which was likewise presented to him on his departure. It was agreed, at this last interview, that the two armies should separate, and that Nizam should return to his own dominions. This separation was not, however, to take place till after Ayder had taken possession of Vaniambari and Ambour, which he had resolved to besiege. It was likewise settled that Ayder should continue the

---

\* They who have charges in the palace that place them in the household, never sit before the sovereign, however high their dignity (as do the generals, and other persons of distinction) till a prince, the friend and equal of their master, gives them a title. Nizam gave a title to Ayder's high-steward; and Ayder returned the compliment by giving an honourable title to the son of Nizam's nurse, who possessed an employ in his palace.

war againſt Mehemet Ali Khan and the Engliſh; and that Nizam ſhould attack the Engliſh on the ſide of Mazulipatam, to oblige them to divide their forces.

To ſhew the intimacy between Ayder and his family, as well as his manner of conducting himſelf with reſpect to his relations, it will not be amiſs to deſcribe an interview he had with his mother about this time. This lady, who in quality of queen-mother has the right of commanding in the ſeraglio or palace, having received information of the check her ſon had experienced and which no doubt ſhe ſuppoſed more conſiderable than it really was, departed from Ayder Nagar to ſee her ſon in the army, notwithſtanding the inconvenience of travelling an hundred and fifty leagues in the rainy ſeaſon. She made long journies, and arrived at the camp in a few days. When the Nabob, who had been apprized of the queen's departure, was informed of her approach, he left the camp with his whole army, in Savari, or parade. The army met the head of the queen's retinue at a league diſtance from the camp, at which time they halted; and Ayder

der and his son advanced alone on horseback, till they had joined the palanquin of their mother, which was close and covered with muslin. They both inclined as low as they could on their horses, and placing themselves on the right and left of the palanquin, the lady continued her journey, guarded by her son and grandson, and followed by the whole retinue of Ayder. She passed through the middle of Ayder's army, who saluted her as if she had been the prince himself. The retinue of Ayder's mother consisted of about two hundred ladies, mounted on horses and oxen: they were enveloped in large pieces of thick muslin, which prevented even the smallest part of their clothes from being seen. They all went before the palanquin of the queen-mother, which was followed by eight Garris, or small Indian carriages, covered with scarlet cloth, and drawn by large Persian oxen. There were likewise ten elephants, and a number of camels and beasts of burthen. Some European horsemen preceded the women, and marched on one side. All the retinue was surrounded by about six hundred lance-men, having feathers and bells to their lances;

and the horsemen, who preceded and followed the retinue, were about four hundred in number.

It is said, that when this lady was conducted into her tent, Ayder enquired what could have induced her to make so long a journey, especially at a time when the continual rains rendered the roads almost impracticable; and that she answered, "I was desirous, my son, of seeing how you bear the ill fortune you have sustained." The prince having replied, "That if heaven should put him to no greater trial, he should find no difficulty in supporting it:"—Very well then," replied she, "since that is the case, I give thanks to God; and shall immediately return, that I may be no impediment to your operations." Two days after, this lady, having wished her son every kind of prosperity, departed, accompanied by her son and grandson to the place where they had met her.

The first place of encampment of Ayder's army, after the battle of Tirnmaly, was at Singueman. After having rested two days, they passed the Paler, which was much swelled by the rains, and encamped in a plain five leagues

leagues distant from Caveripatnam, and six from Vaniambari. It was in this camp that Tippou Saeb rejoined the army, that the Subas formed their last treaty, and that Ayder received the visit of his mother. The second day after the departure of that lady, the army marched towards Vaniambari: the cavalry and the greatest part of the infantry arrived in good time to reconnoitre the place, which was found susceptible of being approached by favour of the water, hedges, and trees, without the necessity of opening the trenches. For the purpose of the attack, a garden was chosen, in the midst of the inundation, upon a rising ground; on which was constructed, the same night, a battery of twelve pieces of cannon. As this place is not more than three quarters of a league from the pass that leads to Vailour, a body of troops with artillery were sent to take possession of the same. The commandant of Europeans being slightly wounded, Ayder would not permit him to attend the works during the night; but insisted on his going to repose in his tent, while he himself undertook to superintend the workmen.

In consequence of this determination, he passed the night in the battery, seated at the foot of a tree, in spite of the dampness and frequent rain,—exposed to the balls and shot that killed many workmen and officers near him,—and diverting every one by his pleasantries, till the return of the commandant permitted him to retire.

The battery began to fire about six in the morning: and though the service of the cannon was attended with much difficulty, the English fire was soon silenced; and Captain R——, commander of the place, displayed the white flag, and sent Mr. D——, his second in command, to treat about a capitulation. This gentleman being conducted to the European commandant, demanded the same terms as had been granted to the garrison at Caveripatnam. After much altercation, on the repeated orders of Ayder to refuse nothing, the required terms were granted; on condition that the commander of the place, and the other European officers and soldiers, should not serve against Ayder for the space of a year. When these conditions were agreed on, on, Mr. D——, much chagrined at not being treated so favourably as he desired, demanded that Ayder should affix his seal to the capitulation. Ayder being advised that the conference was broke off, and the officer was about to return to his place, came forward, and seating himself by the European commandant upon a cannon, addressed himself to the English deputy: " I am not," said he, " commander of the siege. You demand my seal; I have not my great seal here; but to put an end to all difficulties, I give my small seal into the hands of my commandant:" and pulling his ring from his finger, he gave it to the commanding officer of artillery; saying, " Make what use of this you think proper." The officer made an impression with it at the bottom of the capitulation; and this dispute of self-importance was thus, by the good sense of Ayder, put an end to.

The garrison of this place consisted of one thousand Seapoys, and thirty Europeans: fourteen iron cannon, that had been dismounted for the most part by the cannon of the besiegers, composed all the artillery. Besides these cannon, that were found by the English in the place,

place, two other pieces belonging to the regiment of Seapoys were taken. The place made no great resistance, though it was well provided with ammunition and stores, though there was no breach, and a sufficient number of workmen to repair the carriages: but we have already hinted at the reasons that induced the commandants of these places to make so little resistance.

After placing a good garrison in Vaniambari, the army marched towards Ambour, a place famous for the battle gained by the French, and the troops of Mouza Ferring and Chanda Saeb, against Anaverdi Khan, father of Maffous Khan and Mehemet Ali, who lost his life, at the age of eighty-two years, on the third day of the battle, after having repelled the enemy from his retrenchments for two successive days. This place, in which the English had amassed considerable quantities of ammunition and stores, together with artillery, musquets, uniforms, and tents, is composed of three different fortifications, inclosed the one within the other.

The

The first is the citadel, situated on a mountain of the most difficult access, on account of its steepness on all sides. This extensive fortress is capable of containing a numerous garrison, with all the necessary stores, not excepting even beasts of every kind: two very large basons, cut in the rock, contain much more water than it is possible to consume from one rainy season to another: and lastly, the ramparts are constructed with such strength and firmness, that for this reason, as well as the elevation of the mountain, very large cannon, and much time, would be required to make a breach.

At the foot of the citadel, and on the only accessible side, is a fort, which the English have strengthened by the addition of a pallisaded covered way, and a glacis: and lastly, a town of considerable magnitude incloses the fort, defended by a brick wall, with round bastions, and a dry ditch. Half the town is covered from any attack by a large pond; at the end of which the English have constructed a redoubt, which closed the road that led between the pond and the river, and commanded the road

road on the other side between the river and a high mountain.

As soon as the army had encamped about a league distant from Vaniambari, on the banks of the river they had passed at Vaniambari, Ayder went, the very same evening, to reconnoitre the town, in spite of a very heavy rain, that was partly the cause of his being in great danger: for, having advanced to the border of the pond, he found himself unexpectedly exposed to the cannon of the redoubt, which was masqued by trees, and the end of the bank of the pond. This artillery, which consisted of three large pieces, made a discharge that killed fifteen horse, and covered Ayder with blood, and the limbs of the unfortunate men that were slain. Notwithstanding this accident, Ayder continued to reconnoitre the approaches; and resolved to cross the river again with his army, to encamp on the other side of the town; where he should be in a position equally advantageous for the security of his camp, and for prosecuting the siege of Ambour, which would be blocked up by his camp on the side

side of Vailour and Sattgheri, and by the army of Nizam on the side of Vaniambari and Ventigheri.

In consequence of this resolution, the army traversed the river during the night, and passed under the fire of the redoubt before the break of day; so that a few stragglers among the valets and suttlers were the only persons that suffered.

Between the river that flows on the side where Ayder's army was encamped, and a chain of mountains that extend from Ambour to Sattgheri, is a plain about three leagues in length, and of an unequal breadth, from half to three-quarters of a league. One extremity of this is entirely shut up by the town of Ambour, the redoubt, and the river. This part of the town, whose approach was much favoured by fields of a kind of millet, then very high, was judged capable of being taken by storm, without making any breach. Orders were consequently given to prepare ladders of Bamboo \* : but as it was thought that

\* The Bamboo is a kind of large reed, very well known.

that the garrison, which was numerous, might make resistance, the grenadiers and best infantry were ordered to make the attack.

The order of attack being settled, the chiefs of each corps were conducted, in open day, to reconnoitre those places they were destined to march against; and at the close of the evening, after supper, the troops spread themselves in the plain, carrying their ladders, and posted themselves opposite that part of the town they were to assault; with orders to lie down, and wait in silence for the concerted signal. Cannon were likewise conducted into some deserted houses, that formed a village in the midst of a great number of trees, fronting the part nearest the river; from whence it was judged they might favour the attack, by enfilading the rampart. The English, who

---

known. This wood is so useful, and grows so quickly, that it is found every where. It is excellently adapted for scaling-ladders, because it is round, of a requisite thickness, of a very great length, and never breaks. Any utensil may be cut out of it with a pocket-knife, as the wood is as soft as deal.

could

could not be ignorant of thefe preparations, as they were openly made, appeared very bufy during the whole night; and kept a great firing on the village, whofe houfes they fhot through and through, without killing more than one man. They continually threw out fire-pots and fufees, to difcover the manœuvres of the affailants; but while the night lafted, Ayder's troops remained at their eafe. At the break of day they advanced in good order from all parts, carrying their ladders, with drums beating and colours flying, till they came to the edge of the ditch, into which they defcended. They mounted the walls and baftions fo quickly, that Ayder's colours were hoifted on the ramparts immediately after, in fpite of the cannon and mufquetry of the enemy, which was not very fharp; whether it be that the commandant of the place did not think proper to make a longer refiftance, or whether the Englifh had retired, fuppofing the efcalade would not take place. Some men were at firft feen on the baftions; but the cannon placed in the village, or perhaps their fears, drove them away: for the

the grenadiers in afcending found them abandoned, and immediately proceeded to plunder the town. Some of them having ventured to purfue the fugitives as far as the glacis of the fort, found themfelves expofed to a cannonade that deftroyed confiderable numbers; others were flain in the ftreets by the cannon of the fort and citadel, which obliged them to ftretch curtains acrofs the ftreets, and to cut paffages through the houfes. Among thofe who were flain in this attack, was the brave and generous Caki Saeb, Pirjada, or grand almoner, who was running from houfe to houfe, according to his laudable cuftom, to prevent the foldiers from committing any act of cruelty.

Ayder himfelf formed the project of this attack by day; and conducted the left wing of his troops in perfon, on horfeback, with his fabre drawn, to the edge of the ditch.

At the beginning of the night an Englifh gunner, a deferter, gave information that the garrifon of the fort would retreat into the citadel that night, and that they were employed in carrying off the moft valuable effects, and deftroying the reft. The commandant of Europeans

ropeans proposed to Ayder, immediately to attack the fort with all the grenadiers; having the Europeans, as well horsemen as gunners, at their head. This being agreed to, every preparation for the attack was made in an hour; and at eight o'clock the troops sallied forth through the streets, and leaping into the covered way, scaled the fort, which the English made haste to abandon; however, they could not do this so quickly, but that twenty-five Seapoys, an officer, and six Europeans were taken prisoners, two of the latter being wounded.

The English had thrown a large quantity of cartouches into a pond in the middle of the fort, and had caused a fire to be made in the *place d'armes*, for the purpose of burning the uniforms, a considerable quantity of which were saved. The besiegers found eighteen brass cannon designed for field service, three thousand firelocks, a great quantity of shot, bullets, and gun-flints, and a considerable stock of rice and flour. There were likewise store-houses filled with tents, chests, and effects belonging, or intended to be sold, to the army; which was

very

very acceptable plunder for the foldiers; and might eafily have been faved, as Captain C——, commandant of the place, was in a fituation to have defended the fort a very long time, his garrifon being numerous, and well provided both with artillery and ammunition.

The facility Ayder met with in taking all the Englifh places he attacked, encouraged him to undertake the fiege of Ambour; though he had received advice, that the Englifh were marching from all parts to affemble at Vailour. Firm and determined in his fmalleft refolutions, he refufed to follow the prudent advice that was given him, to repair immediately to Vailour; as he eafily might in a fingle march, the diftance from Ambour being only ten leagues. At this laft place he would have been in the centre of the Englifh quarters, which were difperfed for more than forty leagues round, and might have prevented them from uniting; a ftep of fo much the more confequence, as the Englifh at Madras had lately received a reinforcement of troops from Bengal, which the pofition of Ayder's army,

army, at Vailour, would have prevented them from joining the other troops.

The difficulty of taking the citadel of Ambour, which we have described as being situated on a steep mountain, was rendered much greater to Ayder, by the circumstance of his being without either bombs or mortars. The ditches of the town, serving in some respects as trenches, favoured the approaches; and many guns were mounted in a short time, though with the loss of the best gunners, who were uncovered from head to foot, by reason of the elevation of the castle. Ayder allowed but one night for constructing the batteries, and consequently the parapet could not be made of the requisite height and thickness, till after the loss of many brave men. Cannon were planted on a mountain that overlooked the citadel; but the English, in two days, erected a bulwark on that part of the citadel exposed to the ricochet, or rolling shot of the cannon, which rendered them absolutely useless. The great distance between the two places prevented the firing in battery from the mountain; so that after seventeen days siege, with the loss of many Europeans, and much powder and ball, the work was no more advanced than at firſt. In this ſtate of affairs news arrived that the Engliſh army was aſſembled at Vailour, and was preparing to march and raiſe the ſiege.

On this intelligence Ayder took the reſolution of anticipating the enemy, and retreated.

The redoubt we have ſpoken of being entirely cut off from all communication with the fort by the eſcalade of the city, its garriſon conſiſting of one hundred Seapoys, ſix European cannoniers *, and an Engliſh ſerjeant, who commanded, was obliged to ſurrender at diſcretion.

A number of irregular troops being introduced, at the cloſe of day, into the city and fort, who climbed up the ſides of the mountain, and fired upon the guards,—the cannon was drawn off under favour of this noiſe; and at midnight, an hour before the riſing of the moon, all the troops quitted the trenches, and marched to join the reſt of the army that had left

* It is to be obſerved, that in India there are not above three or four Europeans quartered to the largeſt guns, the reſt being Indians.

their

their camp, at the beginning of night, and repaired to another on the road to Vaniambari\*. On the following day the army marched, and encamped on the banks of the river of Vaniambari; its right wing bearing against that fortress, and its front directed towards Ambour.

This retreat of Ayder was the signal of Nizam's separation from him, that Suba retiring into the country of Carpet or Cadapet.

The same day that Ayder pitched his camp at Vaniambari, General Smith arrived at Ambour with his army, consisting of 28,000 men, of which 5,000 were English; for the Bengal

---

\*. A surprising phænomenon happened on the night of this retreat, which was at the end of December: The moon rose at one in the morning; and about three it was so extremely cold, that no one in the armies of the two Subas could remain either in bed or in his tent, though they were provided with carpets and cloth coverlids, but were obliged to light large fires and warm themselves, as in the time of the greatest frosts at Paris. The weather, during this great cold, was very serene, with little or no wind; and nothing similar to it happened on the night following. This event was so uncommon in that climate, that the most aged persons had never known or heard of the like.

reinforcement confifted of fix hundred Europeans, and fix thoufand Seapoys, very much fuperior in appearance to the Seapoys of Madras, and efteemed by the Englifh as the beft infantry in India.

The Englifh general allowed his troops a fhort time for repofe, and left Ambour on the very evening of his arrival, directing his march to Vaniambari.

Ayder was fo confident that the Englifh would not come to feek him, that he did not take the ufual precaution of difpatching advanced guards of cavalry and light troops on the fide of the enemy. There were no other than large bodies of cavalry on the other fide of the river, about half a league from the camp; and two redoubts, raifed about one hundred paces from the fame bank, on an eminence, that ferved as pofts for the advanced guards of infantry. Each of thefe redoubts mounted two pieces of cannon: and it was not till feven in the morning that the approach of the enemy was known by the cannon of the redoubts, that gave the fignal of alarm; at the fame inftant that the arrival of the horfemen put the fact out of doubt.

That which induced Ayder to suppose the English would not pass Ambour, a town on his frontier, was, his having dispatched propositions of peace to the army and to Madras. The bearer of these proposals was an Englishman, formerly factor or consul at Carvac. As the chief preliminary was, that every thing should remain *in statu quo* (an offer so much the more convenient, as neither party had any restitution to make; all the places formerly taken by the English being recaptured, and Ayder having evacuated the dominions of the English, or of Mehemet Ali Khan) he did not doubt of their being accepted. This mediator had promised to send advice, as early as possible, whether he had any hopes of succeeding in his mission. But General Smith, who had his instructions and his projects, did not think himself at liberty to suspend his operations, though he was of opinion that peace would be advantageous to his nation. The Englishman continued his journey to Madras, without sending back advice according to his instructions. On his arrival at Madras, he found the governor and council recovered of their fright, and elated with the hope of succefs from certain intrigues they were carrying on. In this difpofition they treated him as a young man, and derided his propofitions; but the confequences gave them fufficient reafon to repent.

On the news of the enemy's approach, Ayder put himfelf at the head of the piquets of cavalry, and paffed the river; after giving orders to ftrike the camp, to draw up the infantry in order of battle, and to march the heavy artillery and baggage to Caveripatnam; at the fame time commanding his brother Moctum to follow him with all the cavalry.

The Nabob advanced as far as the redoubts. The enemy appeared in good order, coming forward in three columns of infantry: their whole cavalry formed the rear-guard in a fingle line, except two hundred Englifh dragoons, who rode before the columns.

The firft care of this fovereign was to draw off the cannon of the redoubts, and to caufe the advanced guards of infantry to rejoin the reft of the army; and as he obferved that the enemy continued to advance, he
himfelf

himself repassed the river, leaving Moctum Ali Khan at the head of a large body of cavalry, and the commandant of Europeans at the head of the hussars and dragoons, with orders to observe the march of the enemy, and to harrass them even so far as to attack the head of their columns; with the intention of causing them to slacken or stop their march, that Ayder's army might have time to retire. This cavalry, with the dragoons and hussars at their head, hastened to attack the enemy's columns to the centre and the left, which appeared in a situation to come up with Ayder's army the soonest; because the column to the right was on an eminence, and could not pass the river without defiling, as the banks were very steep. The European cavalry were advancing full trot to attack the centre, when several cannon, discharged from the right-hand column on their flank, killed two horses; one of which was that of the commandant of Europeans, who falling, found himself immediately surrounded by the English dragoons, and abandoned by his own, through the treachery

treachery of the greater number, who, together with their officers, gave themselves up to the English. The French commandant, in falling, received a contusion on the buttock and thigh, that formed an abscess; in the cure of which he kept his bed three months at Madras. This desertion stopped the Indian cavalry, who returned; and General Smith ordered his army immediately to halt, suffering Ayder's army to retreat unmolested. A few shot were fired at some cavalry that came to reconnoitre his army, that remained on the same ground till evening, because his equipage could not arrive sooner; at which time he turned back, and encamped on the road to Ambour, about half a league distant from the river.

It is impossible to exceed the politeness and respect that General Smith shewed to his prisoner, the French commandant. He caused him to sleep in his own tent; and informed him, that the march of his army had no other purpose than that of favouring the desertion of the Europeans, which was expected to be much more considerable, in consequence

quence of a plot that had long been carried on, and which they were apprehenfive could be no longer concealed *.

The honour and integrity that the writer of thefe Memoirs has adhered to in the relation of the facts they contain, do not allow him to pafs over in filence the odious plots that were made ufe of, in order to execute this infamous piece of treachery.

After the capture of Caveripatnam, permiffion was given to an adventurer †, a furgeon by profeffion, to retire to the coaft of Coromandel, taking the advantage of going in company with fome Englifh officers, who had been taken in that place. This permiffion was, no doubt, a great indifcretion; but, as the proverb fays, we can never think of every thing; and there was, befides, a

* General Smith did not fire on this troop; and said, that in keeping the fecret, he had forgot to give an order for that purpofe to Colonel Linn, who commanded the column to the right.

† This man, whofe name we conceal on account of his family, has, by his bad conduct, attracted the notice of government, and is now in confinement.

wifh

wish to get rid of a worthless man, from whom there was no reason to fear any thing. Nothing less than an unforeseen chain of circumstances could have given him the power of doing mischief.

This surgeon came to Ayder at Coilmoutour, where he announced himself a Chevalier de St. Louis, and ancient captain of artillery, travelling to Pondicherry. He found credit with the commandant of Ayder's Europeans, to whom he addressed himself; because he had been recommended to that officer by the chief of the French factory at Calicut, who, in forwarding European news, added, *These things may be depended on, as they come from good hands: I have them from M. le Chevalier de * * * * *, who is arrived from Europe by the caravans, and is on his way to Pondicherry, &c. &c.* This commandant did not indulge a doubt respecting the good qualities of the chevalier, who, together with the cross he had the audacity to bear, possessed likewise, to the misfortune of many, an engaging and seductive exterior. On this false appearance of candour and rectitude, the commandant

commandant of Europeans received him in the best manner, and presented him to Ayder, who gave him the command of a battalion of Seapoys, with appointments to the value of four hundred rupees, or £. 50. per month. The man was absolutely without common necessaries; and the French commandant supplied him with lodging, subsistence, a carriage, and every thing becoming a gentleman. After these services, it may naturally be supposed that he would have felt the utmost gratitude and regard for his benefactor: but, on the contrary, his perfidy and want of principle were such, that in less than three months he was dismissed from all his employs. Being on the point of being reduced to beggary, he had the confidence to request permission to exercise his business as a surgeon. This request was made by the mediation of Ayder's surgeon, who had been a fellow-soldier with him in Lally's regiment, and had recollected him perfectly on his arrival; though, at the request of the other, he did not expose him. Our gentleman, thus becoming a surgeon, found himself to be a Chevalier

valier de Chrift \*, by the affiftance of a crofs that ferved every purpofe: it was, however, a real crofs of St. Louis, that fide being untouched on which are the fword and laurel crown, with the motto *Bellicæ virtutis præmium*; but on the other, the enamel that reprefents St. Louis was taken off, and a fmall crofs fubftituted in its place. He affirmed, that he had caufed this crofs to be made in this manner when in Portugal, in order to give it a French appearance. However, he was forbade to wear it; but he adorned himfelf by an embroidery on his clothes, that was permitted him. A fpecimen of his ufual tricks having procured him to be confined, he obtained his enlargement by means of his comrade, with leave to repair to the coaft of Coromandel, in company of fome Englifh officers who were to return to Madras.

\* He affirmed, on the fecond day after his arrival, that he was a knight of this Portuguefe order. The facility with which he conferred thefe dignities upon himfelf, and a long ftay at Lifbon, whence the fear of hanging had induced him to make his efcape, and a patent fince affirmed to be forged, were the caufes why this quality was not called in queftion.

Our

Our adventurer spoke good English, and undertook to court the favour of Captain M * * * * *, by a string of narrations to which that gentleman either gave credit, or pretended to do so. Among other things, he told him, that all the Europeans in Ayder's service, who constituted his chief force, were much disgusted with the service they were engaged in, and still more with their commandant; and that if the government of Madras would employ him, he would engage to cause them all to desert; in the execution of which project, his friend, the surgeon of the Nabob, would engage to lend every assistance in his power.

The English officer, charmed at the discovery of a method of turning the attention of the Madras administration from the cowardly defence he had made, presented our chevalier to Colonel Call, engineer in chief, and a man of great influence in the council. He had great abilities; but, considering the extent of his mind, he was blameable for attending more to the purpose or end he aimed at, than to the difficulties that might prevent his arriving at it. This colonel, who,
like

like many others, was bigotted to the opinion that the Indians can do nothing without the help of the Europeans in their service, was delighted with the project of the chevalier; and presented him to the governor and Mehemet Ali Khan, by whom he was received as a guardian angel. Thus it was that this man, from being a surgeon driven out of Ayder's camp, suddenly found himself the friend and confidant of the governor and Mehemet Ali Khan. He was nobly entertained, and loaded with presents, in spite of the railleries of some Englishmen, who knew him from the reputation he had acquired by exhibiting his tricks at Bengal.

While the gentlemen at Madras were deliberating on the means of carrying their plot into execution, an ancient French officer, of the East India Company's troops of that nation, arrived there. He supposed himself to have been unjustly treated by that Company; and came to offer his services to the English against Ayder Ali Khan.

The project of the chevalier surgeon was communicated to him. He did not hesitate to undertake

undertake the task of carrying it into effect. His offer was accepted, with a promise of making him lieutenant colonel, with the command of a corps in the pay of the English Company; the basis of which was to be composed of the deserters from Ayder.

To engage the confidence of the English government, this officer caused his trunks and valuable effects to be carried to the house of the governor, who placed them in his cabinet. Not to make himself suspected by Ayder, this new emissary repaired to Pondicherry, where he communicated in confidence to all his acquaintance his design of going into the service of that Nabob. A number of officers and young men offered to accompany him. He was careful to transmit their names to the governor of Madras; and left Pondicherry secretly, at the time he expected the complaints of the English governor would arrive. The French governor, on receipt of the letter of complaint, sent for those who were nominated, and demanded their word of honour, that they would not leave Pondicherry without his consent.

The informer, who had the utmost facility in making his journey, because the country he had to traverse was entirely under the government of the English, repaired to the camp of Colonel Wood in the environs of Ahtour. He remained there two days; when that army departing to join General Smith, he went to Ahtour, and declared himself to be French: guides and every thing he demanded were consequently allowed to conduct him to Ayder's camp. He arrived, accompanied by a single servant; and affirmed, that having met the army of Colonel Wood, he had passed two days in the forests, at the risque of being devoured by tygers; and that he had made the journey from Pondicherry to Ahtour on foot.

The reputation he had acquired, probably in consequence of the virtues and talents his relations had exhibited in India, prejudiced the commandant of Ayder's Europeans in his favour. That officer thought himself happy in seeing him arrive, supposing that he had found a companion to share his labours; and consequently endeavoured to render him every

mark

mark of friendship and respect. The emissary at first seemed to meet the advances of the commandant with cordial regard. He waited afterwards on Raza Saeb, whom he had long known, and who reposed the utmost confidence in him on account of his family, which had always been highly attached to that prince's father. Raza Saeb undertook to introduce him to Ayder, who, to the surprize of all present, received him with evident marks of chagrin: which was so much the more strange, as that Nabob always received the commonest French soldier with pleasure. But he had been informed positively by Moctum, his brother-in-law, who had seen the officer at the head of the French cavalry, when he escorted the convoys from Gingi to Pondicherry, that the man was a coward. It was not possible to persuade Ayder to receive him with any mark of respect; as he had too much esteem and friendship for his brother-in-law, not to give credit to his report. By this prevention he could not obtain the command of a company of hussars, that was without a captain and was commanded by a lieutenant who could neither write nor read. The European commandant, not having the least idea of its being possible that a man of family and reputation, as the newly arrived officer was, could deserve such a character, was firmly persuaded that Moctum had prejudiced Ayder against him without reason. To convince him of his esteem, he communicated to him, in confidence, the secret of the expedition against Godelour; believing that he could give him good advice, because he had lately arrived from Pondicherry, which is not more than two leagues distant from Godelour; and expecting that the success of the expedition would be productive of advantage to him. We have already shewn how he made use of Raza Saeb, to frustrate this undertaking; and how he prevented the governor, and the major part of the council, from being made prisoners: for as he knew of the intended expedition of Tippou Saeb by means of Raza, who had an entire confidence in him, he sent off his servant among the Pandaris that Tippou Saeb took with him, because, having no other intention than that of

ravaging

ravaging the country, he could not take a set of men more capable of doing it. The battle of Tirnmaly happened a few days after the arrival of this English emissary; and the officers of cavalry, with the permission of their commandant, who attended his duty as general of the artillery, offered to place him at their head during the battle. But he refused, and kept constantly behind Ayder, who seeing him mounted on a horse of one of the hussars, as he knew by the harness, caused a horse to be presented to him that belonged to one of the Pandaris that had been slain, which was the greatest affront he could shew him.

When the army marched from Singueman to encamp between Caveripatnam and Vaniambari, and had passed the Paler about three leagues from their new camp, the commandant remained with the artillery, on account of the passage being rendered difficult by the rains that had swelled the river. At this time Ayder sent to him, on account of a sedition among the hussars and dragoons, who refused the pay that was offered them as usual, insisting on being paid in silver rupees instead of gold pagodas;

godas; which would have made a difference of about five shillings a month in their favour. As this difficulty had never been made before, the commandant had not much trouble in persuading them to receive the money that was offered them; and taking occasion of the battle lately lost, in which their attack, and still less that of the other cavalry, was not supported so well as might have been expected, he reproached them for raising difficulties about their pay, without shewing any great readiness to deserve it. They who secretly excited them to murmur, were doubtless eager in urging them to resent this affront; for that very evening they went off in a body, with their regimentals and sabres, and repaired with offers of service to the camp of Ram Schander, a Maratta prince, who had received into his pay the Europeans that Ayder had formerly disgraced and cashiered. On the news of their departure, the commandant pursued them at the head of a body of grenadier Seapoys. Ram Schander, cautious of giving offence to Ayder, and probably informed that the Europeans were pursued, ordered

them

them to quit his camp. Being then totally at a lofs what fteps to take, they waited for the commandant, grounded their arms at his command, and fuffered themfelves to be conducted back without refiftance. They were kept bound and expofed to public view for fome days; but at length were reinftated, apparently at the interceffion of Ayder; who did not think it beneath him to pretend to fpeak in their favour. All this may not feem very prudent in Europe; but it is neceffary to attend to the fituation of Ayder and the commandant. Ayder efteemed the Europeans perhaps far beyond their value, and the other exifted only by their means. This fedition was thought to be a kind of bufinefs that would not be attended with any confequences; more efpecially as they did not know where to direct their fteps, or to fituate themfelves better.

This affair happened fome days before the capture of Vaniambari; and every thing feemed quiet, when advices came to the Nabob from Vailour, and from St. Thomas to the commandant, that fome treachery was carrying

ing on, and a desertion projecting, among the Europeans in Ayder's army. Not being able to build any thing upon such general advice, and the agents being such as were least suspected, the commandant supposed he could do nothing better than to assemble all the Europeans, and to require an oath on the cross and the holy gospels, by which they should promise to serve Ayder Ali Khan with fidelity; to advise the prince and the commandant of every thing they might hear to his prejudice; and not to quit his service without asking for permission. Before the oath was administered, every individual was asked whether he had received his pay; and was offered his dismission, if he requested it. This precaution was thought sufficient; and would have been so, if the government of Madras had not employed means to prevent its effect.

The English emissary found an excellent coadjutor in the surgeon, the friend of the Chevalier de Christ: for this man had a natural inclination for hazardous undertakings, and sought to render himself the subject of discourse

discourse at any rate \*. He offered to undertake every thing, on the assurance of being appointed surgeon-major in the English service. But the conspirators not succeeding with the soldiers, on account of the oath they had

* To give an unequivocal proof of the character of this surgeon, it may be recollected, that in 1776 there appeared, in the different journals, a letter pretended to be written by a physician in Sweden, which announced that a man had been delivered of a child, or was at the point of delivery. The singular and ridiculous disputes, on the subject of this phænomenon, are fresh in the memory of every one. The true inventor of this tale was no other than our surgeon, who in 1766 transmitted from Coilmoutour to the Sieur de la G. first counsellor at Pondicherry, the history of this monstrous pregnancy; affirming that Ayder had employed him to act the part of midwife in the business. To his history were added the anatomy and description of the parts, entirely resembling that said to be from Sweden; and as the inventor is in a double capacity the favourite of Apollo, the god of medicine and poesy, he adjoined a poem on the wonders of nature, relative to the prodigy he announced. This history is too well known to admit of the least doubt of its truth.

taken, wrote to Madras; informing their principals that it was necessary they should have the co-operation of the two Jesuits then in Ayder's camp; and that it would be expedient to forward a letter from the governor of Pondicherry to those fathers, ordering the French to quit Ayder's service, by passing over to the army and through the country of the English, who would receive them, and suffer them to join their own standard at Pondicherry.

The Jesuits were in the most absolute state of dependance on the English; and having no other existence in India than they were pleased to grant, they thought themselves obliged to serve them according to the directions transmitted to them. They obtained passports from Ayder for their domestics passing to and from their houses at St. Thomas's; and by that means became the agents of the correspondence of the English with their emissaries. They were provided with a fictitious letter from the governor of Pondicherry, who had already written to Ayder in their favour, supposing them to be prisoners; though they received every kindness, and only waited a favourable opportunity

tunity to return. To perform the commission they had from the English, they privately shewed the Europeans the pretended letter, affirming that they were forbidden to shew it to the commandant; but that the governor had sent to them to excite the Christians to leave the service of a Mahometan prince; at the same time that, as divines, they informed them that their oath given to an infidel was null, and ceased to be obligatory, by reason of the order of the king's representative. The producing a letter of this kind to the soldiers of Ayder cannot be denied; as the fact is notorious, and can be proved by many witnesses now in Paris. The letter was false, because the governor of Pondicherry could have no reason for concealing it from the commandant: on the contrary, that officer being in possession of letters entirely written in the governor's hand, it would have been in his power to have prevented any suspicion of its forgery, if it could have stood that test: and as the governor was not ignorant that a counsellor of Pondicherry had a correspondence in cypher with the commandant, by which

which all difpatches were communicated to him, he would certainly have informed him of the contents of this letter, which was addreffed to all the French in Ayder's army. The Jefuit fathers who ferved the Englifh in this bufinefs, as well as the three Portuguefe priefts, were fent back in company with the Englifh factor, who went to Madras with propofitions of peace.

When the Portuguefe priefts arrived at Vailour, and faw the Jefuits give their letters to General Smith and the governor of the place, they were in the higheft aftonifhment to find that thofe reverend fathers had charged themfelves with a miffion of fuch a nature; and fo much the more, as the news they brought appeared to be not cafual, but early and important. The priefts never fpoke of this event without trepidation and fear; protefting they were innocent, and totally ignorant of the intrigues and manœuvres carried on againft a prince who had loaded them with favours. In fact, Ayder had given each of them, at parting, the fum of three hundred rupees to bear their travelling charges; a fum which is equivalent

valent to thirty guineas; and if he had been so disposed, it was in his power to have inflicted on them the punishment the worthless Jesuits had so well deserved.

Ayder having retired to Caveripatnam, General Smith took possession of Vaniambari, which had been left without a garrison; but he could no longer follow Ayder, because he was obliged to wait for the convoys of ammunition and stores that had a great distance to travel: and the difficulty of collecting a sufficient number of oxen for draught and carriage was such, that he was under the necessity of detaching a part of his army to bring forward the convoy. The capture of the stores and ammunition laid up at Ambour, was the cause of all these delays in General Smith's operations.

The government of Madras, according to their promises, formed a body of light troops, composed of cavalry and infantry, under the name of the foreign corps; of which their French emissary in the camp of Ayder was made commandant, and the Chevalier de Christ commissary. To put a finish to the relation

of

of these detestable proceedings, we think it necessary to mention, in this place, the fate this new troop experienced in spite of the intrigues of the commissary, who employed not only subornation but assassination. To augment the foreign corps, he was always reduced to little or nothing; those who were sent to Pondicherry and elsewhere to enlist men, were discovered; almost all the horsemen deserted, and took refuge either at Pondicherry or with Ayder, who paid them for horses they brought, as if they had not stolen them from himself. The commandant of this unfortunate corps was punished, according to his deserts, by those very men whom he had served at the expence of his honour. An English court-martial declared him a coward, and unworthy to continue in the service; and condemned him to be degraded from his rank, and expelled from the army. We have already mentioned the fate of the Chevalier who first projected this scheme.

Nizam Ali Khan, who, as we have before observed, quitted Ayder, and departed for the country of Carpet, was no sooner arrived there,

there, than his Divan and worthy minister Rocum Daulla wrote to Mehemet Ali Khan, his brother-in-law, to acquaint him that he had at length prevailed on Nizam to abandon Ayder; and that if he and the English desired it, he would repair to Madras, with full power to make such a treaty as they might wish for or expect.

The governor and council of Madras hastened to signify their desire of seeing so great a personage in their capital: and, in consequence, Rocum Daulla and Ram Schander, a Maratta prince, one of the principal confidants of Nizam, repaired with great pomp to Madras, where they made a magnificent entry, being saluted by the cannon, and the English troops lining the streets they passed through. They were every day entertained with new spectacles, and conducted to see the shipping, and every thing that was deserving their attention: but what gave them the most satisfaction was, the valuable presents that were made them. Nizam had the least share; the presents sent to him were of inconsiderable

able value; but the deficiency was made up by promises of vast magnitude: and, on the other hand, these great and magnificent ministers signed a treaty, by which Nizam Daulla confirmed Mehemet Ali Khan in the Nabobship of Arcot, and in all the country he possessed or might obtain. Nizam Ali likewise ratified the gift to the English of the four circars or provinces to the north of Masulipatam, as well as the gift of that great city.

Two counsellors of Madras afterwards departed, in quality of ambassadors, to Nizam Ali, who sent them back with the greatest honours, and loaded with presents for themselves and the governor. Thus it was that this Suba, who, twenty years before, held the destiny of India in his hands, became a kind of beggar among other powers, and daily lost that credit and consideration which gave him his superb titles.

Morarao, a Maratta prince, possessor of a small territory beyond Scirra, joined the English army, bringing with him about two thousand

thousand five hundred horse, and three thousand foot, the whole in bad order; but the English sought for succours from all parts.

General Smith, perfectly acquainted with the nature of the country, and the kind of war he was to carry on, endeavoured without success to prevail on the council at Madras to accept the offers of peace held out by Ayder. He therefore offered it as his opinion, that it would be more advantageous, instead of losing time in making sieges, to pursue and press Ayder's army as much as possible; and, if he could not be come up with, to besiege some place of consequence. He proposed, for the object of their efforts, Benguelour, the capital of a fine country. But the government of Madras, determined to conquer all the country on the exterior side of the grand Gates, obliged the general to divide his army into two parts, and to give the command of one part to Colonel Wood, for the purpose of besieging and taking all the small places that lie in the vallies, while General Smith was employed in keeping Ayder's army in employment.

General

General Smith having complied with these orders, the project appeared to be attended with the greatest success. Colonel Wood took a great number of places, and that with so much the more facility, as three fourths of them had no other garrison than the militia of the country. These conquests wonderfully elated the governor and council, who, as the crowning stroke of their success, received the news that an armament of about eight thousand men from Bombay had landed at Mangalor, and taken that city; whose feeble garrison, not being assisted by the inhabitants, had made their escape. Ayder's vessels, being then at Goa, were not captured; but three hundred pieces of cannon were found in the place, including a quantity of very indifferent iron guns, designed for the shipping, and for the most part unserviceable:—but this is of no consequence, as the number of guns is always a great ornament to a relation. The commandant of this army wrote word, that he intended, as early as possible, to march to Ayder Nagar, not imagining he should find any difficulty

culty in penetrating fo far, and ftill farther from indulging a doubt of taking it, together with the immenfe treafures Ayder had laid up in the place.

This important piece of news was announced to the people by one hundred and one cannon fired from Fort St. George; and the relation of the capture of Mangalor was fpread into all the European fettlements, and every other part of the country.

The news of the landing of the Englifh at Mangalor had been inftantly forwarded to Ayder: he was confequently under the neceffity of haftening to oppofe this army, that had taken footing in the centre of Canara, a kingdom lately fubjected to him, and which he fuppofing, from its fituation, to be out of the reach of infult, had not provided with any confiderable number of troops.

The troops that had been left at Bifnagar, Scirra, and Syringpatnam, received orders to march immediately for the kingdom of Canara. The fon of Ayder had the advanced guard, at the head of three thoufand cavalry; and Ayder himfelf marched with three thousand of his grenadiers, part of his artillery, and about twelve hundred of his cavalry, leaving the rest of his army under the command of Moctum, with injunctions to harrass the two English armies for the purpose of retarding their operations, but to hazard nothing.

General Smith, as soon as he was apprized of the departure of Ayder, proposed again the siege of Benguelour. The council, elated with the high expectations they had built on the news from Mangalor, were for once of his opinion: but as they regarded the siege of Benguelour as an affair of the greatest importance, it was resolved that Colonel Call, chief engineer, should have the direction; and to emancipate him from the orders of General Smith, it was ordered that there should be a committee in the army, composed of the Nabob Mehemet Ali Khan, Colonel Call, and Mr. Mackis; the two last being of the council. This committee were, conjointly with General Smith, to decide on all the operations; and in order that such grave personages might not have the mortification to fail in an enterprize

prize of such importance for the English nation, it was determined that the greatest preparations should be made. In consequence, they were furnished with sixteen mortars of different calibres, thirty-three two-and-thirty pounders, fifty smaller cannon, with a profusion of powder and ball, and every other ammunition: and since all these things had a tract of eighty leagues to pass over before they arrived at Benguelour, and the original difficulty of procuring oxen still remained,—several stations were appointed to be waited at till every thing was in sufficient forwardness to begin the siege. General Smith employed himself in securing a passage for the convoys, by the capture of a number of fortresses he found in his way. He even succeeded in taking one small place by stratagem. His scouts had taken an Algara belonging to Moctum, who carried a letter, advising the commandant of that place, that at the close of the night he would receive a reinforcement of five hundred Seapoys; at the same time informing him, that he was in danger of being besieged. General

neral Smith having an Algara * who was perfectly acquainted with the court and army of Ayder, gave him the charge of this letter of Moctum, with orders to carry it to the commandant, and assure him of the arrival of the succours. The letter produced its desired effect. At the close of night they received a body of English Seapoys, who did not fail to take possession of the place.

Moctum being informed of this event, had his revenge a few days after, and retook the place by another stratagem. He caused some Indian horsemen to appear on the plain, among whom were a number in blue uniforms, like the English dragoons. One of them was detached to advise the commandant of the place, in good English, that they were pursued by a large body of Ayder's cavalry, and that he was sent by the commanding officer of

---

* All these Algaras are Bramins; a circumstance that ought to diminish the idea the Europeans have of these men, who are supposed to be all priests and men of learning. They are chiefly employed as couriers or spies.

the detachment, to desire the gates might be kept open for their reception. This man was an English dragoon, who had newly deserted with his horse, which prevented any suspicion from arising. A large body of cavalry appeared, and the pretended English detachment came full speed into the place, took possession of one of the gates, and admitted the whole troop. The horsemen in blue were clothed with the habits of Ayder's cannoniers.

Colonel Wood besieging great numbers of places, according to his instructions, found himself very soon in a considerable embarrassment for want of troops. He accordingly wrote to the council at Madras for reinforcements, observing that his troops were dispersed in garrisoning the different places he had taken; adding, that, if it was their pleasure that he should destroy these places instead of garrisoning them, it would be necessary to supply him with a large quantity of powder for that purpose. While he was in expectation of the answer of the council, he besieged Darmapuri, a place somewhat more considerable confiderable than thofe he had hitherto attacked. The commandant was a brave man, named Pinda Khan, highly efteemed by Ayder, and formerly in the fervice of the French. This active commander made a vigorous defence, and did not hoift the white flag till the breach was made, and the ditch filled. His deputies having waited on Colonel Wood, he offered them no other capitulation than that of furrendering at difcretion. The deputies not being authorized to accept fuch hard terms, without confulting the commandant, returned to the place; almoft all the garrifon being then on the rampart and in the breach. When they faw the deputies return, they crowded about them, to enquire what fuccefs they had met with; and at the fame inftant the Englifh grenadiers leaped out of the trench, mounted the breach, followed by the Seapoys who had been commanded for the affault, and all the garrifon, the commandant, his fon, and every officer, were inhumanly maffacred; except twelve European cannoniers, who were faved by the Englifh grenadiers. This affault was made

while

while the white flag was on the breach. It is reported that Colonel Wood's army was enraged to find no plunder in all the places they had taken: for Ayder had commanded all the inhabitants of any place in danger of being besieged, to leave the same with all their effects; and had strictly forbidden the officers and soldiers from having any plate or valuable property, but only the small quantity of linen which is absolutely necessary in India. In this order he observed, that the Europeans make war on the Indians only in hopes of plunder; and that it was not proper to indulge their avidity.

It is not easy to determine why Colonel Wood and his officers did not repress the cruelty of the soldiers, since they avowed that the grenadiers made this attack without their orders.

To revenge the sufferers at Damapuri, Moctum afterwards massacred a considerable body of Seapoys in the plain of Ovilour: and as for Ayder, he conceived so violent a hatred for Colonel Wood, that he always afterwards endeavoured, in preference, to attack his army, and to lay snares for him;

and it is probable that the confequences would have been very difagreeable to that gentleman, if he had unfortunately fallen into the hands of Ayder.

After the capture of Damapuri, Colonel Wood joined his army to that of General Smith, according to the orders he had received from Madras. That general, after fecuring the paffage of his convoys, marched towards Benguelour, and took feveral neighbouring places: among others were Colar and Ofcota; and with the intention of making this laft place the ftorehoufe for the fiege, he caufed it to be fortified.

On his approach to Ofcota, General Smith received a deputation from the inhabitants of Divanelli, who came to offer him a contribution. They informed him that the fmall town, and its fortefs or caftle, were the places that had the good fortune to fee the birth of Ayder Ali Khan; a circumftance that had affured them of the favour of that prince, who had beftowed many privileges on the town and territory. General Smith replied that he fhould be the firft in giving the example

of

of respecting the birth-place of so great a sovereign; and granted safe-guards as well for the town as the territory of Divanelli. He refused to accept their contribution, and strictly forbade any individual of his army from entering the place without his permission.

This proceeding augmented the esteem Ayder had long conceived for General Smith: and on this occasion that sovereign sent two superb horses to him, as a present he begged him to accept.

The commander of the army from Bombay, who supposed, after the capture of Mangalor, that nothing now remained, as he wrote to Madras, but to march to Ayder Nagar, found his expectations not a little abated, when he was informed that he had sixty leagues to travel in a country intersected by woods, mountains, and rivers, and more especially that the approach to Nagar would be attended with the greatest difficulty. He did not, however, give up his intention; but continued his preparations, though very slowly. His army was then encamped without

out the gates of Mangalour, in the greatest security.

The son of Ayder marched from Benguelour with all the ardour of a young man, who burns with a desire for glory. He quickly arrived in the kingdom of Canara, whose people, alarmed, but full of confidence in the son of their king, ran before him as to the man on whom their safety depended. Animated by the acclamations of the people, the young prince continued his way to Mangalor, causing all the troops to follow him that he found in his way, and who assembled from all parts. His march was so rapid, and the fidelity of the Canarins was such, that he came in sight of the English camp before they had received any advice. He perceived the tumult and fear his sudden appearance had made. Without waiting for repose after his fatiguing march, he advanced, drove back the guards, attacked the army, totally routed and pursued them to the gates of Mangalor, where his cavalry entered pell-mell with the fugitives. Three thousand infantry, just come up, were astonished to find the

the English camp abandoned. They plundered the camp and the town of every thing they found; which the prince allowed, to punish the inhabitants for refusing to assist in the defence of the city. The route of this English army was so great, that very few had time to make their escape on board the ships, to which they communicated their fears. Their flight added to the ardour of Ayder's Europeans and Seapoys, who immediately embarked and took three transports.

In this manner was the whole English army taken, consisting of the general, forty-six officers, six hundred and eighty English troops, and above six thousand Seapoys, together with all their arms and baggage. This glorious event for Ayder happened the eighth day after the capture of Mangalor. It is difficult to conceive how a victory of this nature could be gained; or how, during the space of thirty days, the English general could neglect the taking possession of some advanced posts, which would have given him advice of the approach of the enemy.

Ayder

Ayder arrived the evening after the victory; and his son had nothing to say but, with Cæsar, *veni, vidi, vici*. It is said he wept for joy when he embraced his son. Some Portuguese merchants, established for several generations at Mangalor, entertained the opinion, that from the fortunate disembarkment of the English army, and the great successes that the English attributed to General Smith and Colonel Wood, it was probable that the English would conquer the greatest part of Ayder's dominions, or at least remain masters of Mangalor. They had therefore the imprudence to treat with the English general, and to contract with him for supplying the army with provisions. As soon as Ayder was informed of this circumstance, he caused these merchants to appear before him, with the chief of the Portuguese factory, and several Christian priests belonging to the three churches at Mangalor. He then demanded of the Portuguese chief and the priests, what punishment the Christians inflict on those who should presume to betray their sovereign, by giving assistance to his enemies. The Portuguese

guese officer having without hesitation answered, that such a crime deserved death; Ayder replied, "I do not judge in that manner, for our laws are milder. Since they have made themselves English by engaging to serve them, their property shall be adjudged to belong to Englishmen; and themselves shall be thrown into prison till I make peace with that nation." Ayder, after this decision, hastened to return to the kingdom of Benguelour, taking care to leave a strong garrison at Mangalor.

During Ayder's expedition and return, General Smith had sufficient time to receive his artillery and ammunition. Mehemet Ali, and the other commissioners of the council, were likewise arrived with a numerous suite, and with a new kind of luxury, unknown till then even in the armies of the Indians: this, however, consisted in nothing else than a number of large covered waggons, loaded with a provision of all sorts of wines. But after all these preparations, it was discovered that the rice and provisions were in so small a quantity, that they could not possibly hold out the

the time the siege might probably last; while Ayder and his troops would not fail to recover part of the fortresses that were to secure the convoys from the country of Arcot. And it was, besides, impossible to send escorts strong enough to defend them against the army of Ayder; General Smith having need of all his troops, as well for the siege, as for the defence of Ofcota, where his stores were deposited, and to keep an open communication between the two places.

Morarao proposed to make the siege of Ciota Ballapour, otherwise Little Ballapour, a strong fortress about ten leagues from Benguelour, and three leagues from the country of the Patane Nabobs; as he affirmed that, when they were masters of Ballapour, he could obtain, either from his own dominions, or from Sanour and the neighbouring countries, any quantity of rice or sheep that they might desire. This advice being approved of by the committee, General Smith left Ofcota with his army, and every necessary for making the siege of Ballapour. He left a strong garrison in Ofcota;
where

where Mehemet Ali Khan, Colonel Call, and Mr. Mackis were to remain.

Ayder, who had followed General Smith, and continually harraſſed him with his cavalry and ſometimes with his artillery, perceived that he could not prevent his opening his trenches before Ballapour: he therefore raiſed his camp, and marched for Oſcota, where he arrived a little before day. As ſoon as dawn appeared, he attacked and carried the ſuburb of the place, which was defended by a ſingle retrenchment of earth, and a ditch the Engliſh had made: he took a conſiderable number of ſoldiers and Seapoys the Engliſh had placed in an hoſpital there; and, deſirous of intimidating Mehemet Ali Khan, whoſe puſillanimous character he was well appriſed of, he ordered his troops to prepare ladders for ſcaling the ramparts of the place, himſelf animating and giving money to the workmen, and promiſing the higheſt rewards to his army if the town ſhould be taken, and Mehemet Ali Khan made priſoner. The view of all theſe preparations, and the reports of ſome priſoners who were ſuffered to eſcape

escape for that purpose, terrified Mehemet Ali Khan in such a manner, that, in spite of every thing that Colonel Call could urge, it was decided that an order should be sent to General Smith, to raise the siege of Ballapour, which was already far advanced, and come to the relief of Oscota. The general, to whom the danger of Oscota had been magnified, was obliged to comply with this order, though so very prejudicial to his operations. Mehemet Ali Khan was encouraged by the return of General Smith; but was determined to run no more risk of falling into the hands of Ayder, but to return without delay to Madras. Colonel Call's colleague was of the same opinion; and General Smith alone not being a committee of the council, was obliged to follow them; and that more especially, as nothing less than his whole army was necessary to escort them. They were under the necessity, at their departure, of leaving at Oscota all that immense quantity of artillery and ammunition that was intended to overthrow Benguelour.

Ayder

Ayder gave himself very little trouble to retake the number of places that were garrisoned by the English, but contented himself with following their army, and harrassing it; which he did in so vigorous a manner, that the terror of Mehemet Ali was not a little augmented.

It was during the time that General Smith marched against Ballapour, that Ayder had the satisfaction of beholding the return of his brother-in-law, Mirza Ali Khan, whose defection had so sensibly afflicted him. This young man, whether from the natural goodness of his heart, or from the contempt shewn him by Madurao, the Maratta general, and the other chiefs of that nation,—was continually agitated by remorse for his past conduct; and had long reflected on the means of regaining the friendship of his brother-in-law. But when he saw him abandoned by Nizam, attacked by General Smith on the side of Benguelour, and obliged to hasten with his son to defend the centre of his dominions, attacked by another English army; when he reflected that all the misfortunes of his brother-in-law, in-law, the friend and protector of his youth, might with justice be attributed to his ingratitude, his remorse was too keen to admit of longer deliberation. He made levies of troops, quickly placed himself at the head of twenty thousand men, and traversing the kingdoms of Scirra and Mayssour, arrived within two leagues of Ayder's camp. Attended by a few horsemen, he advanced to the outposts, where he announced his name, and requested to speak with Moctum. Moctum, astonished at so unexpected a message, hastened to meet him. " What has brought you here?" demanded Moctum with an earnest emotion, when he saw the young prince. — " Repentance," replied Mirza; " I come to repair as much as is in my power the injury I have done to our brother. I bring a much better army than I deprived him of; and I offer my head to his mercy: bring me to him." It was in vain that Moctum represented that it would be proper to advise Ayder of his arrival.— " No," exclaimed Mirza; " bring me to my injured brother: I fear no consequences but those of not seeing him." Moctum told him

him to follow him, and they soon arrived at the tent of Ayder. The young prince threw himself at Ayder's feet, who raised him, and embracing him—" This is no surprize to me, Mirza," said Ayder; " I have long expected thee." The two armies joined; and every one esteemed this return of Mirza as a happy presage of the return of Ayder's good fortune.

Ayder, after following the army of General Smith as far as Vailour, changed entirely his manner of making war. He divided his cavalry into three bodies; of which he himself took one, and gave the command of the other two to Moctum and Mirza, his brothers-in-law: he kept no other troops but his grenadiers, his Caleros, and Carnates, which he likewise divided into three, between himself and his brothers-in-law, so as to form three flying camps. These light armies traversed the whole country, spreading terror and disorder every where, and throwing the council and all the English settlements into the greatest consternation. This was a subject of great pleasantry and satisfaction to all the other Europeans in India, moſt of whom they had inſulted in the ſhort period of their proſperity *. By their quick movements the three armies ſeemed to be multiplied; and the news of their appearance arriving from all parts, it was impoſſible to determine which way to face; and General Smith's army made a number of uſeleſs movements, that harraſſed his troops without finding the enemy.

The council determining to divide their army after the manner of Ayder, a body of troops under Colonel Frichman, a Swiſs, who had never yet been engaged in ſervice againſt the Nabob, was entirely cut off; he himſelf,

---

* They had demanded that the French deſerters, who had arrived at Pondicherry, ſhould be given up, together with the horſes they had ſtolen from Ayder.

They had threatened the government of Tranquebar; and had forced them to give up an emiſſary they had ſent to entice away the men of their garriſon.

They had compelled the governor of Paliacate, a Dutch fort, to deliver up a Frenchman who had taken refuge in that fortreſs, and had obtained their protection.

as

as it is said, alone escaping by the swiftness of his horse. This colonel was marching in a plain, surrounded on three sides with wood: his army, at most about four thousand men, of which six hundred were Europeans, marched in a long column, when some horsemen appeared at the bottom of the plain. Several of the officers represented to the colonel, that Ayder's cavalry was habituated to make sudden attacks at full speed; and that it would be proper to close the column, and approach the wood, in order to support themselves against it. The colonel laughed at this advice: " Be easy," said he, " you shall see how I will serve these Negroes." The number of horsemen increasing, and no one daring to speak to the colonel, all on a sudden a cloud of dust appeared: the colonel then attempted to give his orders, but there was no time. Three thousand horsemen fell on his little army, and every thing was in disorder in an instant. The colonel, in the general confusion, hastened to fly: he was pursued, and the goodness of his horse alone preserved him. Moctum, enraged at the massacre

sacre of Darmapuri, suffered his horsemen to act with unrestrained fury. Above fifty English officers were slain, or made prisoners. Captain R———*, who had surrendered Vaniambari, and had engaged not to serve for a year, was taken. It was more than ten months that he had signed the capitulation. He was, as it were, compelled by the governor of Madras to go with his garrison of Seapoys to garrison in Madura, and was on his march with Colonel Frichman. Moctum, on whom these reasons made no impression, having found him marching in the body of the army, caused him to be hung on a tree, after having refused the other officers the permission to ask his life of Ayder. All these events happened in 1768.

In 1769, Ayder, on his side, being employed in following Colonel Wood, who commanded a body of seven or eight thousand men, and being very near Thiagar, succeeded in falling upon his rear-guard, and forced him

* A colonel of Seapoys ranks as captain of Europeans.

to retire into a wood. This colonel was then endeavouring to throw a garrison into a place named Elvanissour. The commandant he had nominated was the captain who stood first in the order of seniority; a brave man, but subject to the vice of drinking to such an excess, as often to render him incapable of giving any orders: however, not to disgrace him, and with the persuasion that Ayder would never undertake the siege, Colonel Wood suffered him to possess the charge. It so happened, notwithstanding, that the Nabob came before the place with some cavalry, a few hundred grenadiers, and some small pieces of cannon, without either the means or the intention of making a siege. The captain commandant, absolutely intoxicated, mounted his horse, caused the gate to be opened, and rode directly towards Ayder's troops, demanding to see the Nabob. Being conducted to the prince, he represented to him that he was governor of the place, and regarded it as an honour to be besieged by so great a sovereign; that he hoped to deserve his applause by making a brave defence; but that he and his garrison having

having neither wine nor arrack, he had come, in reliance on his great reputation, to beg he would either give or sell them a provision of both, that they might be enabled by their brave defence to give him a new occasion of acquiring glory. Ayder, supposing him to be insane, and not believing him to be the governor of the place, promised to supply him with wine and arrack, presenting him with various sorts to taste; so that the captain in a short time was under the necessity of being carried to bed. While he slept off his wine, he was shewn to several people of the town, and they all knew him. On his waking he was informed, that, as he had entered their camp as a spy, it was a decided thing that he should be hanged; but that, if he was really governor of the place, he might give an order to surrender it to Ayder, it being left to his choice, either to give the order or to be hanged. The poor man obeyed, and signed the order; and, what is still more extraordinary, the commanding officer under him obeyed the order, and opened the gates. In this manner Ayder took a place, with a regiment

regiment of Seapoys, by the ignorance of him who obeyed the order, by the drunkenness of him who gave it, and still more by the imprudence of Colonel Wood. During the time these affairs were transacting, the son of Ayder and Mirz Fesoulla Khan, under whose command the greatest part of the infantry and artillery were, busied themselves in retaking those places the English had garrisoned; and in fact they retook them all, except Oscota, in which were a strong garrison, and a fine train of artillery, that Ayder hoped to obtain by a treaty of peace.

While the ravages, the success, and the rapid movements of the Nabob held the governor and council in perplexity, a vessel arrived from England with Mr. Dupré, ancient counsellor of Madras, and esteemed a man of great sense and understanding. He was sent out to take the government of that place on the first of January 1770, and arrived early in March 1769. He had orders for the governor and council of Madras to make peace on any terms.

The Company were weary of attending to the flattering hopes of conquests that were promised in the letters from Madras. Instead of the diamonds and treasures of Ayder, they saw nothing arrive from Madras but bills of exchange, drawn on them by the government of that place: they therefore thought it their interest to make peace with Ayder at any price, if for no other reason than to prevent the fall of their stock. But it is the great defect of all companies, that even their most essential deliberations cannot be kept secret. The resolution that any power takes to solicit peace, ought above all things to be concealed; and the axiom, *Si vis pacem, para bellum*, deserves the utmost attention. The Company's envoy signified and declared, that a messenger must be dispatched to Ayder to request peace. The person charged with this mission received for answer, " I am coming to the gates of Madras, and I will there listen to the propositions the governor and council may have to make." This answer was taken for a declaration, that the Nabob was determined to besiege the town. Preparations were consequently

quently made, and orders given to the two armies to unite and encamp near Madras.

Ayder Ali Khan continuing his movements, came near Pondicherry and Godelour, and advanced as far as Collentz, seven leagues from Madras on the Pondicherry road. The English army prepared to defend the passage of the river of St. Thomas, when Ayder suddenly disappeared, and while all the world was at a loss to determine where he was, he all at once shewed himself at the gates of Madras on the Paliacat side, and dispatched a flag of truce to demand what propositions they had to make. The whole town was instantly in an alarm, the English army being a league and half on the other side. The council deputed Messrs. Dupré and Boschier, the one appointed governor for the year 1770, and the other brother to the then governor. They were received with great politeness. A suspension of arms was agreed on for the environs of Madras only. Ayder promised to establish his quarters on St. Thomas's mount; and on the 15th of April 1769, two treaties were signed to the following effect:

In

In the first, which is in the name of the king of England, it is agreed, that there shall be peace and friendship between George III. king of Great Britain, &c. and Ayder Ali Khan Suba of Scirra, &c. and their respective subjects; that all the prisoners shall be given up on both sides; and that there shall be an absolute liberty of commerce between the subjects, and in all the dominions, of the two sovereigns, in the same manner as before the commencement of hostilities.

The second treaty between Ayder and Mehemet Ali Khan implied, first, that Mehemet Ali Khan should immediately evacuate the town and fortress of Oscota, which should remain in the same state as at the signing of the treaty; that all the artillery, arms, and ammunition whatsoever should be delivered to Ayder *; and the garrison should retire into the country of Arcot by the

---

* The state of the artillery and ammunition has been given in a former page. It may here be added, that six thousand firelocks were also found in the place.

shortest

shortest road. Secondly, That Mehemet Ali Khan should annually pay a tribute of six lacks of rupees, of which the first year's revenue should be paid down. Thirdly, That all the families of the princes, and other persons of distinction, formerly established in the country of Arcot, and then prisoners, should be set at large, and be at liberty to reside where they pleased.

The other articles of this treaty are not interesting.

The English Company engaged themselves for the performance of this, and promised to present Ayder Ali Khan with a fifty-gun ship *, instead of that which had been seized at Bombay, and was become unfit for service. The Company likewise engaged to supply Ayder with twelve hundred Europeans to serve in his army as often as he should demand it. An engagement of the same nature

---

* This ship was given in 1772 or 1773. It is said that it was a new ship, finely painted and gilt, with all its cannon of brass; but that it was built in such a manner, as to be unfit for any use but parade in a harbour.

was already subsisting between the Company and Nizam Daulla, Suba of Decan.

The council of Madras made the most superb presents to Ayder; and that prince, in return, presented them with much more valuable effects, both in gold and silver. The two treaties were made to save the honour of the king and English nation; and consequently the first treaty only was made public by authority. But as there is always an opposition wherever there is an English government, the second treaty was soon made public in England and elsewhere; with such annotations as the interests or opinions of individuals might lead them to make.

Colonel Call, the principal author of the last war, was one of those who most formally opposed the present treaty. General Smith, who had given his opinion for peace whenever Ayder proposed it, being persuaded that it might be concluded on with credit to his country, was, however, against the present peace. He urged, that it was out of the power of Ayder to do any future injury to the English, since it was in his power to prevent that Nabob from undertaking any siege: and he added, that there was no doubt but Ayder would be the first to give up a war he could not continue with any advantage; more especially as his truce with the Marattas expired at the end of the current year; and the prince was too intelligent not to be desirous of finishing the present war before he engaged in another. So that by holding out a short time longer, and refusing his propositions with the same haughtiness as they were made with, he would be forced to recur to those he had made after the siege of Ambour. To all these reasons he joined, that, in signing a shameful treaty with Ayder, they would dishonour the English name, that had never yet received a blemish in any of their wars with the Indians.

We shall finish the history of this war by describing a print, that shews, with considerable accuracy, the different sentiments of those who were then at the head of the Madras government.

There was fixed to the gate of Fort St. George, called the Royal Gate, a design, in which

which was seen Ayder Ali Khan seated under a canopy, upon a pile of cannon; Mr. Dupré and the other ambassador being on their knees before him. Ayder held in his right hand the nose * of Mr. Dupré, drawn in the form of an elephant's trunk, which he shook for the purpose of making him vomit guineas and pagodas, that were seen issuing from the mouth of this plenipotentiary. In the back ground appeared Fort St. George; and on one of the bastions, the governor and council were drawn on their knees, holding out their hands to the Nabob. On one side of the council, was a large mastiff growling at Ayder, the letters J. C. (for John Call) being marked on his collar; and behind the mastiff stood a little French dog, busily employed licking his posteriors. This last animal was adorned with a star, such as the Chevalier de Christ, Colonel Call's confidant, wore. At a distance were seen the English camp, and General Smith holding

* This gentleman is dignified with a nose of an enormous magnitude.

the treaty of peace in his hand, and breaking his sword.

By this peace, Ayder Ali Khan gloriously finished a war, which all India supposed would terminate in his ruin.

When Ayder quitted Madras, he marched by the way of Oscota and Benguelour, to dispose of all the artillery and ammunition which the garrison of the former place were commanded to deliver to him. After taking possession of the whole, he dispersed his troops into good quarters, that they might refresh themselves, and be of good service to him in the approaching war with the Marattas, which he knew to be inevitable.

The Marattas suppose they have a legitimate right to one fifth part of the revenue of certain parts of Indostan, by virtue of a gift made them by Aurengzebe. Ayder, as we have already observed *, does not acknowledge this claim. He gives money to the Marattas when the necessity of his affairs does not permit him to refuse it; but he

---

* See the note, vol. i. p. 192.

never makes any other treaty with them than a truce for three years, not chufing to own the legitimacy of their demand; and the Marattas themfelves are better fatisfied with this mode of adjuftment, than to continue the war at the rifque of being forced to abandon their claim.

Madurao, who was not then arrived at his two-and-twentieth year, and already poffeffed all the qualities that form the hero, was far from wifhing to confent to any thing that could prejudice the honour and interefts of his nation. He burned with the defire of oppofing himfelf alone againft Ayder. In confequence of the different fentiments of the two warriors, the greateft preparations were made on both fides; and the Marattas, as ufual, came into the field in November, and approached Scirra in the month of December. They found Ayder Ali Khan encamped near that city; and in fpite of all the ardour and courage of Madurao, the pofition of the Nabob appeared fo refpectable that he durft not attack him. But the Marattas being in poffeffion of Maggheri and Mark Scirra, places

acquired

acquired by the defection of Mirza, had the facility to spread themselves in the plain of Mayssour. Ayder was obliged to follow them, and to encamp on the island of Syringpatnam, which he had newly fortified, and put under the command of Mirr Fesoulla Khan, with a good body of infantry. As he returned from Scirra by Bisnagar, and kept near the mountains that cover the kingdom of Canara, he covered that kingdom, and could not be surrounded in his march to Syringpatnam, though the Marattas harrassed him continually.

Very early in the year 1770, Ayder arrived in the island, and was in perfect security from the Marattas. He suffered them to traverse the country, which he had not laid waste as he did when their nation had joined the English and Nizam Ali. He had no apprehension that the Marattas would employ themselves in sieges like the English; and he relied on the generosity of Madurao, whom he knew to be incapable of destroying for the sole pleasure of doing mischief; that general suffering his troops

troops only to forage, and plunder the flat country, according to their cuſtom.

The Maratta army was compoſed of two hundred thouſand men, of which above one hundred thouſand were cavalry. Againſt ſuch an army Ayder riſqued much if he loſt a battle, and could gain little by deſtroying a part of them. The Nabob therefore continued in his camp, notwithſtanding many feints and temptations that were held out to him by the Maratta general. At length this young warrior pretended to retire, and take the road to the kingdom of Benguelour. Ayder thought he might with advantage follow the enemy in a country that was very favourable to his infantry, who were much ſuperior to thoſe of Madurao. He had already marched nine leagues, and hoped that very evening to gain a covered country, where it would be in his power to gain advantageous poſitions, as well for the purpoſe of harraſſing the Marattas in his turn, as for the eaſy ſubſiſtence of his army. But the Marattas having briſkly returned, obliged him to encamp in a place, where

where indeed he was in no danger of being attacked, but where the enemy entirely invested him, and cut off his communication and means of subsistence from all sides; so that he was obliged to quit his camp, and retire towards Syringpatnam. The Maratta army appeared to direct their care and attention to prevent him from following the road to the kingdom of Benguelour and the neighbouring mountains, while they left the road to Syringpatnam free. Ayder chusing the night, as the most favourable to his infantry, deposited the greatest part of his artillery and baggage in a fortress, against which he had pitched his camp *; and at about eleven at night he began his march in a square battalion. His infantry was formed into two columns, and his cavalry at the head and rear closed the square, in the centre of which was the baggage, and the artillery at each end.

* The Author of the present History was in India at the time of this event; but was not a witness of this stratagem of the Marattas. He gives the recital as he had it from an officer of distinction in Ayder's army on the spot.

This order of marching did not admit of much expedition; but he had already advanced more than three leagues by four in the morning, when it appeared that they were not purfued, and that probably the Maratta army was unapprized of their march. There were not then more than two leagues to be traverfed, before they would arrive at a camp where they might fafely remain till night; and one fingle night would have been fufficient to have brought them to Syringpatnam. Every one fuppofed that nothing was to be feared, when a numerous corps of cavalry, confifting of about twelve thoufand horfe, appeared drawn up in order of battle, not behind them as expected, but in front to oppofe their march. Ayder ordered the march to be continued, making ufe of the artillery only to oblige the enemy's cavalry to give way. The cannonade appeared to fucceed, and the army marched forward, though flowly; when at day-break the whole Maratta cavalry appeared, and in a fhort time furrounded Ayder's army. The enemy made feveral charges, which were well fuftained and repulfed: but

Mirza,

Mirza, who commanded the cavalry in the van, suffered himself to be hurried away by his eagerness to follow the enemy he had repulsed. He quickly attempted to return, for fear of leaving the infantry without defence; but the cavalry he pursued were close at his heels, and entered the battalion with him. In an instant every thing is in the greatest disorder; the army is beaten and dispersed; Ayder Ali Khan is himself wounded, and many of his friends slain, and among others Ali Jami Khan, Nabob of Vendevachi. Almost all the troops threw down their arms. A single battalion of grenadier Topasses formed themselves into a close column, and made way by their fire to an eminence, where their commander * died of his wounds. This battalion

---

* He was a native of Westphalia, who had acquired almost all the languages of India. The Author of this History took him into his service as an interpreter. He was afterwards made captain of grenadier Topasses, at the formation of that body of troops. He died gloriously at the head of his battalion.

talion was led to Syringpatnam by a young officer, who was wounded in the shoulder, and was the only surviving officer of the corps.

Ayder, after running the greatest risques, arrived at his camp with the entire loss of his army, artillery, baggage, ammunition, and colours. As it is not customary in India to make prisoners of common soldiers, or even subaltern officers, the greatest part returned to him, though without horses or arms; but, by means of his resources, Ayder established his army, in a short time, in a better state than before. It will scarcely be credited that he purchased again of the Marattas themselves the greatest part of the arms and horses they had taken from him: but this arises from the nature of their government, which is purely feodal, every man having a right to dispose of his share of the plunder as he thinks proper.

lion. His name was Lené. —— The young officer is a Maltese; his name is Mammou. The Author introduced him to Ayder.

Madurao,

Madurao, however, embraced this occasion to begin the formation of a body of Seapoys, with the musquets that fell to his share after the defeat of Ayder's army.

Many French officers lately arrived were present at this battle, simply as volunteers: they were almost all wounded, and one was killed. M. Hughel, who had formerly served Ayder as commander of the French cavalry from Pondicherry, was wounded, and afterwards died at Tranquebar in consequence of his wounds.

There were likewise several English officers present; and among them Colonel Stewart, who arrested Lord Pigot, and who was reported to have been slain in the present war, in the first battle between Ayder and General Coote.

After this battle Ayder kept constantly within his camp at Syringpatnam; and the greater number of the Maratta chiefs having left the army, on account of their six months service being expired, Madurao renewed the truce with Ayder, who was obliged to open his purse upon the occasion, though he had
promised

promised himself the contrary. This truce was made in July 1771; but it was for no more than a year.

Mirza Ali Khan, who, as we have observed, was the cause of the loss of this battle, was taken prisoner, and conducted to Madurao, who addressed him thus, " Since you have made war upon us with the power we have given you, we should act properly if we were to take every thing from you, and confine you for life; yet, however, if you will swear never to bear arms against the Marattas, I will restore your dominions and your liberty." Mirza took the oath without hesitation; and Madurao having set him at liberty, he departed to his small state, where he made an absolute donation of all his property, dominions, and troops to his brother-in-law Ayder; and a few days after became a Fakir, which in Persian signifies a mendicant, a man who voluntarily embraces poverty.—This class of men make no vows, in which respect they differ from monks, who cannot quit their state; neither do they, like them, live in communities. He wrote to his brother-

brother-in-law the reasons that induced him to take this resolution, informing him that he saw no other means of preserving what he had consecrated to his service; and assuring him that if circumstances should in future point out occasions for him to be useful, he should always be ready, however dangerous the service. And, in fact, when Ayder is at war with any other enemies than the Marattas, Mirza takes arms and follows the camp, as he does in the present war against the English.

Ayder employed this short time in producing divisions among the Marattas; and from thence arose the catastrophe that deprived young Madurao of life, to the extreme grief of Ayder.

Raguba, uncle of Madurao, having performed the functions of general during the minority of his nephew, beheld himself, not without great pain, reduced to the state of an individual, after he had secured the dignity that devolved of course to his nephew. During his regency he had filled all India with his fame, and obliged the emperor of the Mogols

gols to fly from Dehli, his capital, which he had destroyed and plundered in such a manner as perhaps never to recover its former splendour; while the emperor himself, by that event, became reduced to a mere phantom, possessing no more than the shadow of the power, the riches, and the grandeur of the ancient emperors.

Madurao, young, ambitious, and elated with his increasing reputation, disdained to listen to the counsels of his uncle Raguba and the other chiefs of his party, which induced the old general to contrive plots for his destruction. Madurao having determined to carry the war into the environs of Dehli, and on the Ganges, found much opposition in the national council: his opinion however prevailed, and he marched with a powerful army at the end of November 1772, leaving a considerable force in the hands of a Maratta general, named Goupalrao, to carry on the war with Ayder Ali Khan. The army of this general was not at all comparable to that of Madurao when he made war in Mayssour; he therefore suffered Ayder to recover Mark Scirra

Scirra and Maggheri, which produced a suspicion that he was either intimidated by the arms, or gained by the bribes, of that potentate.

Madurao did not meet with all the success in the north of Indostan that he had expected, and marched his army back into the Maratta country. During his march there were many seditions among his troops, most probably in consequence of a plot contrived against the young prince: he was found assassinated in his tent in the year 1773, before his arrival at Poni, the usual residence of the general of the Marattas. As he left only one son, an infant, his uncle Raguba assumed the regency by his own proper authority. The cruel and unexpected death of the young Madurao, who was beloved by his soldiers, gave rise to suspicions among the principal chiefs that Raguba was either the author or accomplice of the assassination of his nephew. A conspiracy almost universal being formed against him, he attempted to collect and form an army of the troops in which he could place most confidence; but he had scarcely began his

his march against his enemies, when the greatest part of his soldiers left him. Perceiving himself abandoned, he had only time to take refuge among the English at Bombay, who received him with open arms, and promised him assistance. In return for this support, he thought proper to make a treaty, by which he granted very advantageous concessions to the English nation; and among others, never to demand the Chotay, or one fifth part of the revenue of all the lands the English might possess in Indostan.

On the news of this treaty being forwarded to the government at Bengal, General Goddard was dispatched from the banks of the Ganges with an army of eight thousand men, twelve hundred being Europeans. With this force he crossed the peninsula, marching about six hundred leagues, in spite of all the petty princes whose dominions he traversed, and at length arrived at the banks of the Sindi or Indus. He found that the Marattas, after having surrounded the Bombay forces commanded by the governor of that island, had forced him to capitulate; and that the governor had promised to abandon Raguba, to interfere no more in the affairs of the Maratta nation, and had annulled the treaty made with the fugitive general. This last event happened in 1774.

General Goddard, without waiting for any orders, declared the capitulation, as well as the consequent treaty signed by the governor of Bombay, to be null and void. Thus the war commenced again; and this general, who if he had belonged to any other power would have been criminated, had the good fortune to see his audacity crowned by many victories, which however finished by obliging him to act only on the defensive, his successes even destroying his army, and the Marattas seeming to multiply in consequence of their defeats; because they were defending their own homes, and their country is exceeding populous.

Ayder, who, as we have before observed, had fomented the troubles that agitated the Maratta nation, took, at the beginning, the part of Raguba (which assuredly he would not

not have done, if he had had only that war to support). In confequence of this proceeding, after the defeat of the regent and the Bombay army, feveral Maratta chiefs, who fupported the party of Raguba, and among them Goupalrao, were forced to throw themfelves into his protection. He furnifhed them with troops, and taking advantage of the diftraction of the Maratta nation, in confequence of the victories of General Goddard, he took a number of their ftrong places, which now form a fecond barrier beyond Scirra, Maggheri, and Mark Scirra. Though the greateft number of thefe places are of great ftrength, and advantageoufly pofted, yet the moft part were taken by fimple blockade; which occafioned Ayder to employ feveral years in this war. He did not think proper to take more vigorous meafures, for fear of obliging the Maratta nation to accommodate their difference with the Englifh; which, however, was a very difficult thing to be brought about, on account of the horror and averfion that people had conceived againft Raguba.

In

In the year 1775, Ayder, profiting by the employment the English gave the Marattas in the defence of their own possessions, embraced the opportunity of sending a small army, under Cina Serrao, a Maratta lord, who had served him from his infancy, to punish the Samorin, and other princes of the Malabar coast. This prince refused to pay the tribute he had consented to give, when Ayder, in 1767, restored his dominions. The Samorin, fearing the anger of the Nabob, thought to secure himself by offering to become a vassal to the crown of France. The commandant of Mahé accepted the gift of the Samorin, and came with a few troops to take possession of the fortress of Calicut, where he hoisted the French standard. This was a most imprudent and inconsiderate step, for many reasons.

First, the commandant of Mahé had not forces sufficient to sustain the consequences of this act; the number of troops on the Mahé establishment not being more than one hundred and fifty men.

Secondly,

Secondly, he ought not to have made an agreement in the name of the French king, without first being authorized by the commandant general of the French establishments in India.

Thirdly, he could not but know that Ayder Ali Khan was reputed the natural ally of France; and that the Nabob had claims on the whole country of the Nayres, by an authentic treaty, concluded by the mediation of his predecessor at Mahé.

Cina Serrao, Ayder's general, paid all the respect to the French colours which his positive orders to take possession of Calicut permitted him to shew. But he gave advice to his master of all that had passed; and the latter having written to the commandant-general at Pondicherry, the commandant at Mahé was recalled, and Ayder's troops took possession of Calicut, which, as well as the rest of the Malabar coast, has ever since remained under the power of that prince.

Ayder being informed, in the month of August 1778, that hostilities had commenced between England and France, made a truce of of six years with the Marattas, by which they suffered him to retain all his conquests. The time required for the conclusion of this treaty, and the great distance between the Maratta frontier and the Nabobship of Arcot, did not permit Ayder to arrive in time to prevent the capture of Pondicherry, which surrendered in the month of October. The Nabob not having arrived on the frontiers before the month of November, laid siege to Chiteldrouc, whose lord or Paleagar being a vassal of Maysfour, was encouraged by the promise of support from the English to refuse obedience to the orders of Ayder. This place surrendered at the beginning of January 1779. During the siege, Ayder announced to all India the project he had formed of attacking the English. His principal invitation was to induce Nizam Daulla to attack them to the north of Mazulipatnam, in order to recover the four provinces they had extorted from him. The Suba promised to make the attack that was proposed to him; but, whether from timidity or the intrigues of the English, he did not keep his promise, but calmly suffered Ayder to bear all the dangers of the war, and to enjoy, without the participation of any other sovereign, the glory of being the liberator of India.

We can give no details of the operations of Ayder in the present war, having no other materials than the relations of the English; and on these we can place no dependance, because they are fabricated in India to deceive the English government, and afterwards arranged in Europe according to circumstances, and the necessity of imposing on the people. So that the only thing that bears the appearance of truth, is a letter from General Coote, in which we see that Ayder is master of the Company; that in November 1781 he blockaded four places at once; that General Coote marched with his army from Madras to supply those places with provisions, without accomplishing his purpose as effectually as the necessity of the case demanded; that the difficulty of subsisting his army obliged him to bring it back into the environs of Madras; that in his marches his troops had always been harrassed by the cavalry and artillery of Ayder;

Ayder; that he had fought four obstinate battles with Ayder, and gained the field, without speaking of his having taken either prisoners, colours, or standards: to all which he adds, that he sends Colonel Crawford, who will explain the true state of affairs. It may be concluded from this letter, that the English are engaged in a most ruinous war, and that, with the assistance of the French, it may be hoped this prince will succeed in taking possession of the whole Nabobship of Arcot, to which his son has so just a title by the gift of Nizam, as has been shewn.

The direct news from Ayder's army gives an account of the capture of Chiteldrouc, and the particulars of a council held before they entered the country of Arcot. It was deliberated whether he should attack the English, or wait till the landing of the French forces. The latter it seems was the general opinion, and even that of the European officers; but his son Tippou Saeb was of the contrary opinion, and remonstrated that the Nabob had threatened so much to attack the English, that his reputation necessarily required him to proceed.

Tippou

Tippou Saeb spoke with so much spirit and animation, that he was joined by the whole council. It was this young prince who decided the battle that was attended with the deaths of the Colonels Baillie and Fletcher, by taking advantage of the disorder the English army was thrown into by the blowing up of their ammunition waggons, to fall on them with his cavalry. The total defeat of a detachment commanded by Colonel Brawlie is likewise an exploit of Tippou Saeb; who having began, like Alexander, to gain battles at the age of eighteen, continues to march in the steps of that Grecian hero, whom he may one day resemble as well by the heroism of his actions as by the multiplicity of his conquests. As to Ayder, we may compare him to Philip of Macedon, who formed the troops that procured the numerous victories of his son, and subdued the Greeks his neighbours, who were the enemies that were the most difficult to conquer.

THE END.

www.ingramcontent.com/pod-product-compliance
Lightning Source LLC
Chambersburg PA
CBHW032230230426
43666CB00033B/1657